Marianne M. Jennings
Professor Emeritus of Legal and Ethical Studies in Business
Arizona State University, Tempe

Ethics and Financial Markets: The Role of the Analyst

RESEARCH FOUNDATION
OF CFA INSTITUTE

Statement of Purpose

The Research Foundation of CFA Institute is a not-for-profit organization established to promote the development and dissemination of relevant research for investment practitioners worldwide.

ISBN 978-1-934667-61-3

9 September 2013

Ethics and Financial Markets: The Role of the Analyst

Marianne M. Jennings
Professor Emeritus of Legal and Ethical Studies in Business
Arizona State University, Tempe

The ethical issues that financial professionals face are no different from the ethical issues in any profession—or, indeed, the day-to-day dilemmas we all face. These issues are readily resolved through the use of three simple questions: Does this violate the law? Is this honest? What if I were on the other side? These three basic ethical standards are often complicated, extrapolated, rationalized, refined, and confused as those in the financial markets grapple with what they believe are more complex ethical issues today than in the past. But as this review shows, the ethical issues in the financial markets today are no different from those that managers of money and assets, financial advisers, and analysts have faced over the centuries.

> There are no new sins; the old ones just get more publicity.
>
> *Unattributed*

> As a protection against financial illusion or insanity, memory is far better than law.
>
> *John Kenneth Galbraith,* The Great Crash, *1929*

A review of the history of ethics in financial markets and the related literature points to two conclusions: (1) History does repeat itself, and (2) when analysts depart from three simple questions, complex issues are resolved through a thicket of codes, laws, and regulations that encourage further interpretations and exceptions and cloud ethical judgment. The three questions are, Does this violate the law? Is this honest? What if I were on the other side? The last is a question that tends to elicit the simplest summation for ethical missteps: That's not fair! Regulation almost always follows ethical lapses in financial markets, but ethical lapses continue after the regulation. This pattern can be observed again and again. History's ultimate utility is instruction. Understanding what has gone before us provides an opportunity, through knowledge and perspective, to avoid a repeat of past ethical missteps—complex and otherwise—by investment market professionals. The lessons to be found in the evolution of ethics in financial markets lead us back to the freedom and clarity of simple ethical choices, with a resulting opportunity for preserving and advancing trust in the market and enhancing the reputation of its professionals.

Fact patterns change over time; ethical issues remain the same. The ethical issues faced by financial analysts result from the same tension that is present in all professions. Whether lawyer, physician, auditor, architect, actuary, or analyst, a professional has a fiduciary duty that encompasses doing what is best for the client or patient (Bauman 1980). Professionals also must weigh the unforgiving economic requirements, however, such as meeting payroll, that come from operating a business (Ellis 2011). Cash flow does not accept meeting lofty ethical standards of professionalism as an exception to its demands. When ethical dilemmas arise, professionals must struggle to aid one side in their ethical tug of war at the expense of the other. The recognition of that underlying struggle brings all of the ethical issues faced by financial market professionals into perspective. The tension is resolved through attention not to detailed fact patterns but to three basic questions: Does this violate the law? Is this honest? If I were on the other side, would I cry out, "That's not fair"?

The same tensions, questions, and simple answers emerge in a review of the literature related to both investment market ethics in general and ethical issues that have resulted in negative headlines, prosecutions, and settlements with investors. The recurring nature of investment market ethical issues can be seen through a historical review of market collapses in various eras that raised concerns about the ethics of market professionals. In each era, legal and regulatory reforms were passed in the hope that they would remedy what had gone wrong ethically in the market. Instead, unethical conduct similar to what had gone before returned following each regulatory reform. There is nothing new or different in the behavior of investment professionals in 2012 that we have not seen since 2000 BCE. The seemingly complex ethical issues have always been with us, and investment professionals have been down the same ethical paths, more accurately labeled cul-de-sacs, more than once, with what are, in historical perspective, predictable outcomes. The fact that history keeps repeating itself is overlooked with each new law, regulation, or code change. Through legal and regulatory reforms, we attempt solutions that are a mile deep in details and even wider in scope. In the thickets of codes and regulations, however, we are missing what is necessary to prevent financial market debacles from repeating: a reliance on simple ethical principles and concepts.

Readers should note that this review focuses on the ethical dilemmas faced by *security analysts* in contrast to other types of investment professionals, such as portfolio managers, traders, financial planners, and pension plan sponsors. One reason for this focus is that, historically, analysts have been at the center of a large number of revealing and colorful stories involving ethics, not that analysts are less (or more) ethical than others in the investment business. Indeed, as the investment industry has grown, analysts have become less central to it and other professional categories have increased in importance. Thus, no doubt, these other categories will face their proportionate share of ethical dilemmas in the future.

This review is offered with the hope that it will cause reflection on the simple question, What should we be doing differently? Prevention of investment market ethical missteps requires knowledge of the history of financial markets. A review of the past is a necessary step for the kind of ethical progress that will enhance trust in financial markets. An understanding of this history will provide a foundation for moving forward. Given what we learn from history and failed regulation, how do we restore trust in and the reputation of financial professionals and our markets?

Hammurabi, Leviticus, and Ezekiel

Ethics in the marketplace is not a new concept. In fact, fraud has been and always will be with us. The Code of Hammurabi for ancient Babylon (c. 1800 BCE) covered everything from adultery to business trade. The code's basic goal was the imposition of harm on the perpetrator of code violations equivalent to any harm done to the customer or client. For example, contractors had to experience the same fate as the owners of homes those contractors built:

> If a builder builds a house for a man and does not make its construction firm, and the house which he has built collapses and causes the death of the owner of the house, the builder shall be put to death. (Prince 1904, p. 1)

Imagine the same principle applied to investment advisers whose clients experienced collapsed investment portfolios—if you lose their money, you lose yours too.

Although we do not have the specifics on the transactions, the Old Testament makes clear that fraud was present in those ages because we find a warning in Leviticus 19:14 that we should not "put a stumbling block before the blind." Yet another caution comes in Leviticus 25:14: "And if thou sell ought unto thy neighbor, or buyest ought of thy neighbour's hand, ye shall not oppress one another" (from the King James Version of the Bible). The modern translation would be that selling short is wrong if you have the inside information that earnings for the company's stock are going to go down. If you are buying stock, it would be the Biblical act of oppressing if you failed to disclose an upcoming merger revealed to you in advance of public disclosure (Leiser 1989).

In the approximately 1,400 years between that warning and the time of the prophet Ezekiel, apparently not much improvement occurred when it came to fraud, for Ezekiel warns, "The people of the land have used oppression, and exercised robbery, and have vexed the poor and needy: Yea, they have oppressed the stranger wrongfully" (King James Version of the Bible, Ezekiel 22:29). Oppression is translated as fraud, and apparently it was a problem during the eras when we did not even have running water. Strangers were taken advantage of by those trying to sell, sell, and sell. Market sophistication changes, but the problem of taking advantage of others is too often still at the root of all collapsed investments.

The Talmud, Rashi, and Rabbi Obadiah Sforno

The Talmud's principles regarding buyer and seller behavior seem surprisingly familiar and could today serve as a framework for what became U.S. federal legislation on securities and the security markets (Leiser 1989):[1]

- Buyers and sellers should speak truthfully and should not conceal facts from each other.
- Buyers and sellers are required to disclose facts that would change the deal (i.e., material facts).
- Those holding positions of trust should avoid self-dealing (think fiduciary duty).
- Taking someone else's property is always wrong.
- People should deal fairly and equitably with one another.

One of the earliest commentators on Leviticus and the Talmud was the French Talmudic scholar and prolific writer Rabbi Solomon Ben Isaac (1040–1105), known as Rashi. His interpretation of the meaning of the stumbling block in front of the blind included two prohibitions: One should not enable another to commit a wrong act, and one should not intentionally give another person bad advice—advice that would cause that person to buy something he or she did not need or that would result in a loss (Pearce, Resnicoff, Sargent, and Wendel 2006). Investment advice fits into the Rashi guidelines.

The final version of the Talmud drew from the Mishnah (the basic law), and there was no greater expert on the Mishnah than Rabbi Obadiah ben Jacob Sforno of Italy (1470–1550). Recognized as one of the first business ethicists, Rabbi Obadiah wrote that fraud occurs in a transaction when one of the parties is at a disadvantage (i.e., one side does not know the true worth of the subject of the transaction but the other side does). Rabbi Obadiah's description is perhaps the first time asymmetrical information has been addressed. Apparently, 16th century Palermo had its share of insider trading. The good

[1]The Talmud was created between 70 and 200 CE.

rabbi's standard would serve as a lay explanation of the U.S. federal definition of insider trading, which occurs when one side has material nonpublic information and the other side lacks it (Rosenberg and Rosenberg 1998).

Tulip Speculation

The story of the founding and growth of the Holland tulip market provides the earliest documented market bubble, that of December 1636 through January 1637. When the tulip was developed, people were enamored by it. They began buying tulips, fields of tulips, and developing tulip bulbs. Not only "spot" (physical) tulips but also tulip futures were traded, including times when physical tulips were no longer available. Like the 21st century mortgage security market in which mortgages that had yet to be written were pooled for securitization and sale, bulbs yet to be developed were sold in 17th century Holland. At the market's peak, one tulip bulb future cost $10,000 in present-day U.S. dollars. Like its 21st century counterpart, this market depended on trust: Investors took the word of those who promised there would be tulip bulbs in the future. The market was only as trustworthy as the honor of those who were selling these derivative tulip instruments (Jennings 2004).

Eventually, investors realized that those who had sold the futures could not possibly deliver the bulbs, and the market collapsed. The impact on Holland's economy has been described by some as centuries long (Dash 2000). The collapse brought the usual finger-pointing at sellers as well as those who developed the concept of tulip futures.

The story of the world's first market bubble is eerily similar to each bubble since then. At a time when investors could have purchased 24 tons of wheat (tangible goods) for the cost of one tulip bulb future, the event illustrates how the drive to succeed in a bull market clouds judgment and compromises honesty.

The South Sea Bubble

The South Sea Bubble of 1720 continues the saga of dysfunctional financial markets. As one scholar has written,

> Commonalities run throughout the history of these early market bubbles. New finance instruments were exploited . . . against a backdrop of developing legal and financial institutions. An understanding of these complex and sophisticated matters lagged significantly. (Day 2008, p. 475)

Lack of understanding of new instruments and lagging legalities were part of the South Sea Bubble. The confusing instruments involved were joint stock shares in companies that were allegedly using the cash raised to refund the national debt of Great Britain. These stock instruments were backed by the crown in a nation that was the world's greatest power. The problem was the exchange rate—how many shares should be given in exchange for how much debt? Whether by accident or design, the number of shares and shareholders was oversubscribed, and those in the market took advantage of the confusion to sell more shares, which were depicted as low-risk investments. Buyers were told that the risk was comparable to that faced by landowners collecting rent. But the debt-refunding companies had based their financial statements and future projections on the assumption that the exchange rate was valid, an assumption that was both material and wrong. (A 21st century analogy is that mortgage-backed securities are only as good as the ability to collect cash flows on the underlying mortgages and the value of the real property securing them.) When the last round of shares was offered (at £1,000), the share prices began to drop, finishing at a price of £200. A national depression resulted.

Condemned as a cause of the market collapse and resulting depression were the "stock-jobbers," those who sold the shares, "decoying the unwary to their ruin by a false prospect of gain, and to part with the gradual profits of their labour for imaginary wealth" (Melville 1921, pp. 24–25). Stock-jobbers were equated with a Trojan horse, "ushered in, and received with great pomp and acclamation, but which was contrived for treachery and destruction" (Melville 1921, pp. 24–25).

The Birth of Wall Street and the Six Percent Club

The institution we call "Wall Street" was born in 1792 through the Buttonwood Agreement by an association of stockbrokers that would eventually develop into the New York Stock & Exchange Board and then into the New York Stock Exchange (NYSE). As Wall Street got under way, so also did the underbelly of the U.S. market. As Lord Hardwicke explained in 1759, "fraud is infinite" and regulations are "perpetually eluded by new schemes which the fertility of man's invention would contrive" (*SEC v. Capital Gains Research Bureau* 1963, footnote 41). Indeed, 1792 brought a new scheme to this new market. William Duer, a plantation owner, partnered with Alexander Macomb, a land speculator from Ireland, to create their Six Percent Club (Peck 2011, p. 3). The purpose of the Six Percent Club was to buy 6% of all the bank shares to drive up the price of the shares. The club members would then sell off their shares for a tidy profit. A decline in the economy caused the banks to make fewer loans, however, which reduced profits and, of course, reduced the banks' share prices. Duer and Macomb were left with worthless shares as well as all the debt they owed for the funds borrowed to acquire their 6% interest. So ended the introduction of leveraged share buying. Dreams turned to dust, and Duer and Malcomb went under, taking more banks with them in a time when bailouts were not yet a twinkle in the eyes of elected officials. In the fledgling United States, whose constitution was still being ironed out, the losses experienced by so many at the hands of Duer and Macomb resulted in public outrage that amounted to a cry for morality in markets and a condemnation of the evils that spring from greed (Peck 2011). Even at that time, greed was recognized as being not so good.

Dickens on the Ethics of Investment Markets

Following a visit to the United States, Charles Dickens in 1843 wrote his novel *Martin Chuzzlewit,* a character study of the United States. Dickens offered a scathing indictment of business ethics through tales of an architect who takes tuition from students in exchange for having them do his drafting work, which he then passes off as his own. Moreover, the Chuzzlewit family's insurance business, Anglo-Bengalee Disinterested Loan and Life Assurance Company, was created and funded by a pyramid scheme. Dickens depicts those in the investment business as greedy hucksters, and his novel exposed life insurance fraud in the mid-19th century. Although the novel did not fare well during Dickens' day, it has become a reference point for studies of ethics in investment markets in the United States (Gunz and Jennings 2011).

NYSE Growth and Panics Followed by Hearings

The Gilded Age, roughly 1863–1913, was a time of expansive investment in the infrastructure of the United States (particularly railroads).[2] The railroad boom of the 1860s was followed by the Panic of 1873. The panic resulted from the realization that speculative investments in railroads were worthless. Investors had been taken in by the railroad expansion, and overbuilding resulted. Think real estate speculation (Rhodes 1906). Advisers continued to tout railroad investments, however, long after the overbuilding of tracks and facilities was clear. A problem of overbuilding of facilities used in support of the railroads also arose. The factories and businesses tied to the railroad industry or located around railroad facilities were miles wide in expanse and equally deep in leverage. National City Bank (the precursor to today's Citigroup) touted railroad bonds in ads as follows:

> Every railroad bond we recommend has first been put through a fact-searching test. Only when the facts indicate sound values are we willing to say, "This bond meets our standard—we recommend it." (Perino 2010, p. 182)

Yet, the bonds were of junk quality. One historian of the 19th century described the market as follows:

---

[2]The term "Gilded Age" was coined by Mark Twain and Charles Dudley Warner in *The Gilded Age: A Tale of Today,* satirizing what they believed to be an era of serious social problems hidden by a thin layer of gold.

> The fact is there had been overtrading—an excessive conversion of circulating capital into fixed capital—but the financial history of our country shows that it is extremely difficult for bankers and traders to know when the danger point has been reached. (Rhodes 1906, p. 106)

When the railroad bubble burst, more than 100 railroads declared bankruptcy. With the nation's prime business now collapsed, a period of unemployment topping 14% set in for what is now sometimes called the "Long Depression" (Fels 1949). Public outrage over the event resulted in a strong vote for the Democrats in the subsequent U.S. federal election.[3] A lasting result was that there was a "general distrust" of Wall Street among investors as well as bank customers (Rhodes 1906, p. 107).

The states did attempt regulation during this time because of the perception that the federal government lacked the authority to regulate financial markets.[4] The first significant state securities law was passed in Kansas in 1911. It was an antifraud statute that resulted in similar laws in other states referred to as "blue sky laws" because they were designed to prevent swindlers who were so bold that they "would sell building lots in the blue sky" (Seligman 2003, p. 44). The goal of the legislation in Kansas and the other states was to provide investors with more complete information than had been available in the past on which to base their investment decisions.

In 1912 and 1913, the general distrust of the public increased with two events that focused on what may have been the first publicly expressed concerns about "too big to fail"—or, perhaps more accurately, "too big to regulate" (Pratt 1905; Tarbell 1904). Congress, led by Arsene Pujo of Louisiana, held hearings in 1913 on what was called the "Money Trust." The concern was the interlocking directorates of railroads and banks. The hearings concluded that these affiliations violated "the fundamental law that no man can serve two masters" (Mizruchi and Hirschman 2010). The conflicts documented by testimony in the hearings revealed a web of interconnection that was later outlawed by the Clayton Act, passed in 1914, which prohibited competing companies from having directors in common. One article described the interconnections as follows:

> The great size of these firms raised considerable concern among critics, but it was more than their size *per se* that caught people's attention. Of even greater note was the extent to which the corporations were connected with one another in a web of cross-cutting affiliations. Morgan and his firm, J.P. Morgan and Company, controlled several of the leading railroads as well as

[3]Although Democratic presidential candidate Samuel J. Tilden won the popular vote in 1876, he was not seated; Republican Rutherford B. Hayes became president following contentions, contested electors, and a deal to end Reconstruction in the South.

[4]Interestingly, the states interpreted the Commerce Clause to mean that the federal government could not regulate securities markets. The broad interpretation giving that power to the federal government did not come until Franklin Roosevelt's presidency.

> U.S. Steel and International Harvester, and Morgan and his ally, George F. Baker, controlled several of the largest New York banks. Meanwhile, Morgan's great rival, John D. Rockefeller, not only controlled the Standard Oil Company and several additional firms, but also was allied with James Stillman, president of the National City Bank. . . . This community of interest was reflected in the proliferation of director interlocks among these firms. Baker alone sat on the boards of thirty-eight different corporations in 1904, including several leading banks. (Mizruchi and Hirschman 2010, pp. 1072–1073)

Following the hearings, Louis Brandeis in 1913 wrote a series of essays for *Harper's Weekly* (subsequently published as a book) that focused on conflicts of interests and the need for disclosure to investors. "Sunlight," wrote Brandeis, "is said to be the best of disinfectants, electric light the most efficient policeman" (Brandeis 1914, ch. 5, p. 1). Brandeis proposed control of commissions in the sale of securities, disclosure of all charges, and provision of an explanation of who is underwriting an offering and the structure of any syndicate underlying the offering. The congressional hearings following the 2008 market crash delved into the same issues regarding investment bank sales of securitized mortgage instruments.

Brandeis concluded, "The investor should know whether his advisor is disinterested." Brandeis included some sample disclosure language for investment banks to let investors know when and how the banks had acquired and/or invested in the securities they were now selling to others (Brandeis, ch. 5, p. 5). Goldman Sachs was similarly questioned by senators about the firm being positioned on both sides of its transactions in mortgage securities.

Ponzi Schemes

Charles Ponzi (1882–1949) left both his mark and his name in the financial markets. Ponzi, perhaps through studies of Dickens' *Martin Chuzzlewit*, understood arbitrage via the pricing disparity in stamps between Spain and the United States. In the 1920s, Ponzi purchased "reply coupons" in Spain for 1 cent but was able to redeem those coupons in the United States for 6 cents. With a net gain of 5 cents per coupon, Ponzi promised his investors a 50% return on their funds—and all within 45 days (Peck 2011).

Ponzi used his investors' funds for cash purchases of the 1 cent reply coupons. He bought as many as he could to earn his 5 cents. The golden goose phenomenon kicked in, however; given the small supply of the coupons, there was too much demand. Ponzi solved the mismatch by paying off his early investors with cash generated from the new entrants, after taking the usual cut that goes for the creator.

In a similar story emerging in the late 1990s, securities broker Bernard Madoff created a fund that would follow the Ponzi pattern with a promise of steady 12% annual returns (Jennings 2009). Madoff took in investors—from high society and Hollywood stars—by using a feeder network that was skeptical but well compensated. Madoff did pay off the early investors after his creator's cut to support his residences in Palm Beach and the Hamptons.

Bull Market Run-Up, Crash, and the Embarrassing Pecora Hearings

The reforms in the equity markets had their beginnings in the Roaring 20s, Black Friday, and the Great Depression.

Investment Trusts. The 1920s, the time of the bull market climb, was the beginning of the investment firm. Companies were no longer raising capital on their own; they were turning to third parties to obtain equity capital. This movement toward third-party capitalization resulted in the sale of shares in investment trusts that drove market growth. The investment trust shares were actually similar to the auction-rate securities that investment banks would sell to clients nearly 100 years later (discussed in the section "The Real Estate/Mortgage Bubble"). Retail investors were assured of the safety of these securities. In fact, investment trust interests were popular with individual investors because sellers and analysts both made promises to buyers about their stability (Jennings 2010a). The very wording, "trust" and, a century later, "mortgage-backed securities," carried an aura of stability, and financial advisers described these entities as conservative investments.

Despite the moniker, the trusts carried tremendous risk. Investors were not privy to full information about the nature of the market. The market value of these trust interests depended on market demand. The material information that investors were missing was that the investment bankers selling the trust interests were fueling the market expansion by driving up the price of the investment trust securities with their initial leveraged purchases. Duer's 1792 model had not gone unnoticed. The bankers' immediate purchase of the trust shares upon their issuance resulted in the perception that these instruments were in demand and priced according to that demand. Once the perception of public demand was driven to new heights through the underwriting banks' original purchases, the trust shares could then be resold to the public for significant gains. With the profit on the resale of the trust interests, the investment firms were able to begin issuing another round of investment trusts, with each trust being more marketable than the last because of growing markets and increasing investor demand. Each new trust fund was also more leveraged than the previous one, however, because the investment banks had to borrow the cash to complete first-round purchases.

State Regulation. By 1927, the NYSE had seen what the Kansas legislature had already seen—the information investors had was neither forthright nor forthcoming. The exchange responded to the need for better disclosure in stock offerings by imposing filing requirements on its members before they would be permitted to list securities for sale on the exchange. Those requirements included details on the capital stock structure of the company, company history, liabilities, properties, and financial statements for five years. Also required were copies of the company's charter and bylaws and an opinion by independent legal counsel on the legality of the corporate structure as well as another opinion by engineers on the condition of properties listed as assets. The standards of the NYSE were referred to by experts as "the leading influence in promoting adequate corporate disclosure" and considered by Adolf Berle to be "the most forward-looking steps in finance taken during the 1925–1929 boom" (Seligman 2003, pp. 46–47). The exchange's framework was used for the structure of the federal regulatory statutes that would follow this boom and eventual crash.

Doubts and a Crash. Just as with the scheme of Duer and Macomb, the leveraged market structure depended on the demand for trust securities, a demand that had to continue to appear insatiable. If one offering fell flat, the intertwined banks and loans would choke on the leverage as the investor pool ended. In March 1929, Paul Cabot, an investment firm manager, warned in an article in the *Atlantic Monthly* that "dishonesty, inattention and inability, and greed" characterized the investment trust market and cautioned that, without publicity and investor education, "disaster and disgrace" were "inevitable" (Bullock 1959, p. 14). Following publication of the Cabot article, the NYSE put a temporary halt on new investment trusts, but it resumed sales once the fear dissipated.

Doubts about the ability of the market to keep going lingered, but in September 1929, Charles E. Mitchell, National City Bank chairman, said that there was "nothing to worry about in the financial situation of the United States" (Perino 2010, p. 182). Almost a century later, words from that same bank's CEO would be eerily similar. Mitchell sailed for Europe and could not be reached when the stock market crashed in October 1929. Investors who had bought into the "safe" investment trusts were left with worthless investments. Those who had lent the money to the investment banks were left with worthless collateral and debtors who lacked not only cash but also assets. The Dow dropped every day, to a total of 89%, from the 1929 peak to the 1932 bottom.

In the summer of 2007, with the mortgage securities market already fraying at the edges, Charles Prince, CEO of Citigroup, offered Mitchell-like reassurance: "As long as the music is playing, you've got to get up and dance. We're still dancing."[5] A year after Prince's statement, Citigroup required a government bailout, and by the fall of 2009, the Dow had dropped 54% from its 2007 peak.

Public Accountability: The Pecora Hearings and Analysts' True Feelings. The post-1929 congressional hearings on the market crash examined the activities of the investment firms as well as the analysts who had touted the investment trust instruments as safe. The Pecora hearings of 1932 represented a turning point in market regulations and a time during which the public was riveted by the disclosures and testimony before the Senate Banking Committee. Ferdinand Pecora was Chief Counsel to the United States Senate Committee on Banking and Currency during its investigation after the market crash. His aggressive questioning and investigation painted a picture of stock manipulation and fraud through analysts' and advisers' imprimatur on these "safe" investments. (J.P. Morgan, Jr., said, following his testimony, that he felt as if he were "a horse thief"; Seligman 2003, p. 31.)

The hearings revealed analyst behavior that would reemerge during the dot-com and mortgage securities bubble. During the 1920's market run-up, one analyst for National City Bank, Victor Schoepperle, had made a "buy" recommendation on Peruvian bonds, as a "safe" investment. Pecora had found information in Schoepperle's files, however, indicating that the government of Peru had a long history of both political instability and defaults. In those files, Schoepperle had written,

> The condition of Government finances [in Peru] is positively distressing. Treasury obligations are almost impossible to collect. Government officials and employees are months in arrears in their salaries, and, as one business man expressed it, the Government Treasury is "flat on its back and gasping for breath." (Seligman 2003, p. 27)

So, based on his research, Schoepperle's private conclusion about the Peruvian bonds was that the "the moral risk was not satisfactory" (Seligman 2003, p. 27). His public recommendation, however, was a "buy," and Pecora confronted him with the inconsistency between his own conclusion documented in his files and his public recommendation.

Schoepperle reconciled his private notes' negativity with National City's positive public recommendations as follows:

> I thought, like a great many others, that I was in a new era. It was an optimistic era in which optimistic interpretations were put on any situation

[5]Mara Der Hovanesian, "Can Citi Regroup?" *BusinessWeek* (19 November 2007):31, 33.

> where the pros were about equal to the cons. (This and the following quotation are from Perino 2010, p. 237.)

He added that there was a chance for National City to earn underwriting fees through a positive recommendation but no further sales if Schoepperle's true opinion emerged.[6] The bad credit, the political risk, and the long history of both were not included in the prospectus for National City's offerings of the Peruvian bonds in 1927. In addition, National City included a disclaimer that any recommendations on the bonds were not "to be construed as representations by us" (Perino 2010, p. 237). By 1931, these Peruvian bonds were selling at less than 7% of their par value (Seligman 2003, p. 10).

By the time the Pecora hearings concluded in May 1934, trust in financial institutions had all but disappeared. With the decline in the market and the revelations of financial misconduct, hysteria peaked: The press reported that one family taped its cash to the chests of its children, believing that to be safer than risking placing the cash in a bank (Perino 2010, p. 242).

Pecora's focus on the ethical and moral character of the businesses and professionals on Wall Street resulted in the most substantial reforms in the market's history (Jarrell 1989, p. 85; Caccese 1997). Pecora used his skill in cross-examination to obtain detailed information on executive compensation (including incentive programs), affiliated organizations and transactions, and the lack of full disclosure in securities materials, including whether the investment bank underwriting the stock held a position in the stock being sold.

Regulatory Reforms. Franklin D. Roosevelt alluded to these Wall Street issues during his 1932 presidential campaign, and he used the evidence from the hearings on the ethical problems in the stock market to promote the need for legislative and regulatory reform of that market. In his March 1933 inaugural address, Roosevelt described Wall Street as incapable of self-regulation and in need of reform:

> [T]he rulers of the exchange of mankind's goods have failed, through their own stubbornness and their own incompetence, have admitted their failure, and abdicated. Practices of the unscrupulous money changers stand indicted in the court of public opinion, rejected by the hearts and minds of men. ...
>
> The money changers have fled from their high seats in the temple of our civilization. We may now restore that temple to the ancient truths. ...
>
> There must be an end to a conduct in banking and in business which too often has given to a sacred trust the likeness of callous and selfish wrongdoing. (Houck 2002, p. 107)

[6]Commission rates on foreign bonds were 14% (Seligman 2003, p. 10).

As a result of the end of the bull market, the 1929 crash, and the revelations in congressional hearings about the conduct of banks, investment professionals, and company executives, Congress passed the Banking Act of 1933 (the Glass–Steagall Act) and the Securities Act of 1933 (for the regulation of primary offerings). These acts were followed by the Securities Exchange Act of 1934 (for regulation of the secondary markets) and the creation of the U.S. Securities Exchange Commission (SEC).

Glass–Steagall, passed during Roosevelt's first 100 days in office, put limits on executives obtaining loans, required banks to sever their security firm affiliates, and stopped investment firms from accepting deposits. These federal laws also codified simple ethical standards, such as full disclosure in primary offering materials (honesty) and advance registration of those materials (disclosure prior to the sale of the securities). The new federal legislation placed controls on the use of inside information; imposed requirements for disclosure of material information, such as earnings reports (remedying the problem of asymmetrical information that resulted from limited access to information about company performance); and provided criminal and civil penalties for violations of the codified standards. Ethical standards that had been disregarded during the market run-up were codified with the hope that breaches would be deterred or controlled through civil and criminal penalties.

In his speech at the dedication of Michigan Law School in 1934, U.S. Supreme Court Justice Harlan Stone said,

> I venture to assert that when the history of the financial era which has just drawn to a close comes to be written, most of its mistakes and its major faults will be ascribed to the failure to observe the fiduciary principle, the precept as old as holy writ, that "a man cannot serve two masters." . . . The loss and suffering inflicted on individuals, the harm done to a social order founded upon business and dependent upon its integrity are incalculable. (Seligman 2003, p. 622)

Investment Market Reforms: Voluntary Action and Professional Ethics

The pain of the Pecora hearings and the new regulatory world for financial markets resulted in a 15-year era, roughly 1934–1959, of introspection for members of the profession. In addition to the negative public perception of analysts and the loss of public trust in the stock market generated by the Pecora hearings, the financial markets experienced unprecedented volatility following the 1929 crash. Ethical and financial vulnerability brought analysts and advisers together in meetings to work toward resolving the issues that were driving the volatility and those that had caused the loss of public trust. Perceptive analysts took the lessons of the 1913 Pujo and 1930s Pecora hearings and embraced an Edgar Allen Poe resolve of "never more." The 20 years of recovery that followed the 1929 crash and the statutory reforms produced great effort toward voluntary reforms by members of the profession, reforms that went beyond the regulatory mandates. These reforms began as a grass-roots movement and eventually expanded into international organizations and voluntary standards for the analyst profession.

In 1925, four Chicago investment analysts (called at the time "statisticians") began meeting for lunch to discuss the issues facing their profession, and the group formalized its organization as the Investment Analyst Society of Chicago. In the 1930s and 1940s, analysts in New York, Toronto, and Boston followed Chicago's lead. Self-regulation took another step forward in 1939 with the creation of the National Association of Securities Dealers (NASD), which was charged with the protection of investors through standards for and enforcement of open and honest conduct of its members under the SEC's oversight. From this time forward, self-regulatory organizations (SROs) would assume an increasing role in market regulation and enforcement. The tension between the embarrassment of high-profile enforcement actions and business interest in building confidence among investors in the existence of remedies and enforcement has always been present in SROs. The small fines that have accompanied SRO enforcement actions continue to remain an issue (Park 2012).

The early years of voluntary analyst meetings resulted in an increase in knowledge dissemination when the New York Society of Security Analysts began publishing *The Analysts Journal* in 1945. The first issue included a debate about the need for analysts to have a professional rating. The journal's articles continued to fuel discussion about professionalism that branched into discussions about the need for a national organization and certification.

By 1947, the city-based groups had decided to form a multinational organization (the United States and Canada were first to be included) to advance their mission, which was "to enhance the professional and ethical standards of the members and others in the investment community" (Morley 1989, p. 41). The national group that resulted was the Financial Analysts Federation (FAF).

The focus of the FAF was not only on enhancing ethical standards. The FAF members also explored the root causes of analyst misbehavior: How could so many investment market participants have misled so many? One of the causal factors that emerged during those informal lunch discussions was that at that time, the investment analyst profession, unlike the medical and legal professions, had no requirements for entry. The number of investment advisers and analysts in the 1920s had increased, but with no educational or certification standards, advisers and analysts with training and education were indistinguishable from people who simply moved from businesses or the trading floor into the new and lucrative career as analysts. The lack of entry, educational, or licensing requirements, the basics of professional standards, left investors to judge for themselves the credibility, knowledge, and experience of those from whom they sought advice (Caccese 1997). In addition, without formal entry requirements or certification, the profession had no mechanism for self-policing the conduct of investment advisers and analysts. The leaders of the FAF recognized not only a need for entry and certification requirements but also a (perhaps even greater) need for *standards* that would spring from a code of ethics and take hold through disciplinary measures for its violation.

Professional Entrance Requirements and a Code of Ethics

The FAF pursued the goal of entry requirements and standards with some expediency because its members recognized that the post–World War II bull market in which they were working presented many of the same ethical challenges that had been present in prior market swings. Even as these goals were pursued, the FAF also dealt with an issue that would help achieve the professionalism and ethical standards it sought—distribution of knowledge to the members (Regan 1987). The FAF created the Institute of Chartered Financial Analysts (ICFA) in 1959 to address these areas.

The ICFA was given the two-pronged assignment of certification and education. The ICFA was charged with developing and keeping current a body of knowledge that would help members understand the issues in the industry. Through *The Analysts Journal,* later called the *Financial Analysts Journal,* knowledge dissemination continued, including articles that addressed ethical issues in investment markets. The ICFA was also given the responsibility of developing a rigorous examination to be required for members who wished to carry the CFA designation following their names. At least 10% of each of the series of required exams focused on ethical issues (Morley 1989).

In 1962, the FAF adopted its first code of ethics and prepared to offer its first professional exam. The code included a clear enforcement tool: Violation of the code resulted in a loss of the CFA designation (Regan 1987). The basic structure of the code was simple:

- CFA charterholders maintain high standards of conduct with the public, clients, employers, employees, associates, and corporate management.
- CFA charterholders give "meticulous" attention to the letter and spirit of the law and cooperate with government agencies, stock exchanges, and industry groups.
- CFA charterholders put client transactions over personal transactions and do not act adversely to the client's interest.

- CFA charterholders make full disclosures of individual and firm interests in their recommendations for purchase or sale.
- CFA charterholders do not compete with their employers.
- CFA charterholders do not pay commissions or fees to another party for recommending their services without full disclosure.
- CFA charterholders exercise care in borrowing material and give full credit; they always avoid plagiarism.
- CFA charterholders use their designation in a professional manner.

Although the tenets may seem simple, these basic ethical principles addressed all the missteps and misdeeds that had been at the heart of the historical controversies and market collapses. These simple tenets have been changed, expounded upon, detailed, and explained through examples throughout the growth and development of the Code of Ethics and Standards of Professional Conduct of the organizations that evolved from the FAF and ICFA—first, the Association for Investment Management and Research; then, CFA Institute. Still, their simplicity is their strength.

The Emergence of Soft Dollars and the Ethical Issues in Their Use

With its founding in 1792, the NYSE imposed minimum commission rates. Brokers were not permitted to discount those rates (Jarrell 1984). As the FAF was proceeding with its efforts to increase both ethics and professionalism in investment markets, the structure of the market was creating different types of ethical issues. An issue that would remain with the investment industry through the present day emerged during the 25-year period of 1950–1975, that of soft dollars.

The practice of paying soft dollars (payments outside the commission rates) began in the 1950s as investment brokers and traders struggled to compete under a regime of fixed, nonnegotiable commission rates that were probably too high (Blume 1993). Interestingly, the brokers found a way to compete on the basis of price even though they were operating in a price-controlled market. The brokers offered investment managers a valuable commodity that could be included in their price-controlled product—in-house research. The idea behind offering this research service as a price grabber was that good research resulted in increased business for the broker providing that research and, when the research and resulting trades served the managers well, created a means for keeping those managers as customers who returned for more information, and as a result, more trades. From the fund managers' perspective, no hard dollars had to be expended to obtain this research, and they got the additional benefit of obtaining access to institutional analysts' views. Such access was important to smaller fund managers who could not afford their own in-house analysts.

Even as this seemingly free offer of research took hold, an ethical issue gnawed at fund managers: Were they compromising their fiduciary duties to their beneficiaries by accepting the free research? Could the nature of free research escalate into something more? For example, one practice that emerged was commission shifting, where one broker would "give up" a portion of the trading commission to another broker who was affiliated with a fund manager in return for additional business. Would these relationships affect objectivity—for example, when managers selected brokers who referred clients to them (Burgunder and Hartmann 1986)?

The use of soft dollars began a series of court cases that found some fund managers in breach of their fiduciary duties and their duty of loyalty.[7] This creative pricing structure also launched a 60-year debate focusing on the role of fund managers, the firms they select for their investors' trades, and how those selections are made.

Commission Deregulation. The dizzying pace of growth in soft dollar services and the ongoing debate about the related ethical issues attracted regulatory attention in addition to the judicial conclusions. In December 1968, because of SEC pressure and the growth of off-exchange markets, the NYSE permitted brokers to discount commissions (the discount was about 7%) on orders that involved more than 1,000 shares (Jarrell 1984). Correspondingly, brokers were permitted to charge more on smaller orders. In 1971, the SEC allowed commission rates for transactions of more than $500,000 to be freely negotiated; the amount was decreased to $300,000 in 1972. The effect of these changes in commission rates was surprisingly small—a reduction of 3.0% from 1968 levels of commissions (Stoll 1979).

In 1975, to ease the soft dollar tension, Congress amended the 1934 Securities Exchange Act to deregulate commission rates on Wall Street.[8] May Day 1975 (as this move was called because of the date of the change) meant that the NYSE price-fixing scheme for commission rates was eliminated. The unintended consequence of the deregulation, however, was that the ethical issues became more acute because pricing differentials still included the formerly unpriced research services. The soft dollar concept was now institutionalized because commissions and research services were bundled together.

---

[7]See *Moses v. Burgin*, 445 F.2d 369 (Mass. 1971) and *Fogel v. Chestnutt*, 533 F.2d 731 (N.Y. 1975).

[8]Securities Acts Amendments of 1975, Pub. L. No. 94-29, 89 Stat. 97, 97–170 (1975); 15 U.S.C §78bb(e).

Changes in federal law did, however, address the ethical concerns for fund managers with regard to the issue of fiduciary duty should they opt to pay a higher commission rate because of the research benefits. Section 28(e) of the Securities Acts Amendments of 1975 provided an ethical imprimatur for soft dollar brokerage relationships:

> No person [who exercises] investment discretion with respect to an account shall be deemed to have . . . breached a fiduciary duty . . . solely by reason of having caused the account to pay a member of an exchange, broker, or dealer an amount of commission . . . in excess of the amount of commission another member of an exchange . . . would have charged . . . if such person determined in good faith that [it] was reasonable in relation to the value of the brokerage and research services provided. . . [15 U.S.C. § 78bb(e)]

Fund managers now had most of their ethical questions about their fiduciary duty in whether to use soft dollars answered for them by this language (Burgunder and Hartmann 1986). The statutory pass on ethical introspection led to greater use of soft dollar research and other benefits.

Brokers maintained that the managers' beneficiaries received lower trade costs because of the value of the research. Managers argued that it would cost investors more to have the research done independently by third parties than it did to use the brokers' research. Academics reached differing conclusions about whether the soft dollar arrangements actually helped beneficiaries, and the ethical debates continued.

Remaining Ethical Issues. A false security accompanied moving forward under the guise of statutory authority, however, because the bundling of research and commission rates into one fee raised additional ethical issues. One issue was the latitude granted in interpreting "research services."

The definition of research services was wide in terms of what fund managers were actually receiving in their bundled products (Jennings 2007). An unanticipated expansion occurred in the permissible use of soft dollars for the benefit of fund managers. What emerged were "perks" classified as research and paid for with soft dollars. Office furniture, supplies, travel, and other amenities came to be considered research services.

Exacerbating the problems presented by this broad definition was the fact that brokers further distinguished their product with fund managers through a sort of frequent flier program—the more trades fund managers gave to brokers, the more soft dollar research services the fund managers received in return. This combination of built-in, albeit conflicted, loyalty to a particular broker introduced an additional conflict of interest between, on the one hand, what was arguably prudent use of certain brokers for their research and trading expertise and, on the other hand, the personal temptation of choosing a broker because that broker offered the fund manager more perks.

Soft dollar research and soft dollar perks, however defined, were either not disclosed to beneficiaries or were so unclearly defined that it was impossible for fund beneficiaries to determine whether the fund manager's use of a particular broker was in the beneficiaries' best interests. Research and analysis bundled into singular commission rates resulted in an opaqueness to the fees and to the nature of the relationships between fund manager and broker. Fund managers have the responsibility of making investment decisions based on their expertise and research and then authorizing trades based on that research. The soft dollar brokerage arrangement shifted part of the managers' responsibilities to the broker, who was motivated by commissions from trades authorized by the fund manager. Yet, the broker furnished the research upon which investment decisions (trades) were made. A fund manager's decision to change from one broker/trader to another could not be evaluated simply by comparing commission rates because soft dollar research services were built into the commission rates. A higher commission might be justified because of the bundled services and fees, but information was insufficient for beneficiaries to make that determination.

The basic ethical issue in both the price-controlled and open-pricing eras is and always has been a conflict of interest. The services and pricing have continued despite the inherent conflicts because of a comfortable reliance on the wisdom of fund managers in exercising their discretion in obtaining these services and statutory limitations on the definition of "research services." Even with these constraints and statutory protection for fiduciary duty standards, however, conflicts of interests remained.

These conflicts of interests existed because the conflicts in the soft dollar situation were not one-sided; that is, parallel conflicts existed in the broker's *sources* of research. Research comes from three sources: analysts employed by the investment management firm to manage given funds (sometimes called "buy-side analysts"); independent analysts (third parties with no relationship to the fund, its managers, or the broker/trader); and analysts employed by full-service broker/traders (sometimes called "sell-side analysts"). This last group passes its research to fund managers in exchange for commissions directed to the brokerage firms where they are employed. Even buy-side analysts often rely on broker/trader research as a supplement to their work. So, an investment management firm does not avoid conflicts simply by hiring its own analysts.

Independent analysts have to be paid and, in the case of soft dollar bundling, are paid by the broker. These third-party analysts depend on repeat business from brokers and understand that their livelihood depends on the brokers meeting their goals of increasing trading activity and thus commissions. Could third-party analysts be influenced in their research by a desire to please the broker so as to continue their paid relationship? Independent analysts offered their assurance that they were not influenced by the brokers, but the fact that they had to assert their independence is evidence of a conflict, not of its absence.

Finally, the analyst employed by the full-service broker is an employee of the same firm that executes the investment manager's trades. In too many cases, research by employee analysts was influenced by the impact of the analyst's research conclusions on the company's client base and trade revenues. Moreover, the analysts' performance evaluations often included factors related to the revenues that their analyses brought to their employers through soft dollars. For the employee analyst, yet another layer to the complex interrelationships emerged when the broker also filled the role of investment banker as an underwriter for stock offerings. The analysts employed by the underwriter were making purchase recommendations on stock offerings and initial public offerings (IPOs) being handled by their employers. This conflict of interest was exacerbated by the pressure of internal politics and the analysts' performance evaluations (Moses 2004).

The immediate effect of the elimination of fixed commission rates was a 25% reduction in commission fees (Jarrell 1984). Despite the obvious and immediate benefits of the regulatory change, soft dollar ethical questions remained a focus for investment markets for the next three decades. Both anecdotal and empirical research documents the continuing debate on the benefits and detriments of soft dollar fee arrangements.

Public Perception of Investment Market Ethics

A 1980 study sponsored by the Financial Analysts Research Foundation (now the Research Foundation of CFA Institute) concluded that research analysts, portfolio managers, and the supervisors of both groups of people believed that, by and large, financial analysts are committed to "the professionalism of their practice, to the maintenance of high standards of conduct, and to the protection of the public interest" (Veit and Murphy 1996, pp. 1288–1289).

In the years following the release of the study, however, two issues arose that appeared to belie the findings. The first was that public perception and concern about investment professionals was different from the 1980 self-reported perceptions. A 1986 survey found that the public rated brokerage firms and banks as among the most mistrusted of 22 types of institutions, and more than two-thirds of consumers believed that those who provide financial advice put their self-interest ahead of client interests. Included in the 22 institutions were politicians and attorneys (Veit and Murphy 1996). In addition, the greatest economic concern for the public was "ethics in the securities markets." The research documented a disconnect between the profession's perception of its work and the public's regard for that profession.

The public distrust reflected in the 1980 AIMR (Association for Investment Management and Research; renamed CFA Institute in 2004) survey was prescient because the 1980s was a decade of headlines pointing out ethical lapses in the financial markets. For example, from 1980 through 1990, a debate flourished in the literature regarding the need for analysts to have nonpublic information because of their unique role in the markets (Langevoort 1990). As the debate on inside information raged, the 1983 SEC case against Raymond Dirks, a noted analyst, grabbed the headlines, raised ethical issues in the profession, and exacerbated the public's poor perception of analysts.

The SEC vs. Dirks, Role of Analysts in Market-Moving Information, and Groundwork for Expert Networks. The case against Raymond Dirks reaches back to events in the late 1960s and early 1970s. Dirks was an officer of Delafield Childs, a New York broker/dealer firm that had a clientele of institutional investors. He specialized in providing investment analysis of insurance company securities for those institutional investors. Ronald Secrist, who was by then a former officer of Equity Funding, something of a hot stock at the time, told Dirks that the assets of Equity Funding were "vastly overstated" as a result of fraud. Secrist also explained to Dirks that regulators had ignored his pleas for help. The allegations Secrist brought to Dirks were, as the court described them, "incredible" and were offered without documentation (*Dirks v. SEC II* 1982). According to Secrist, one of Equity Funding's subsidiaries had

> created false insurance policies and records to inflate its sales figures, . . . was selling partnerships in nonexistent real estate, . . . its top officers had Mafia connections which they used to threaten the lives of employees who objected to the fabrications, and . . . the accounting firm of Haskins & Sells had dropped the Equity Funding account out of disagreement with the company's business practices. (*Dirks v. SEC* 1983, p. 830)

Secrist had already visited the New York State Insurance Commissioner, information that was passed along to the California Insurance Department and the Los Angeles office of the SEC. The SEC indicated that it had received reports from disgruntled employees in the past (as early as 1971) and recommended that any action on Equity Funding be delayed until the SEC had more personnel available for an investigation.

Based on his conversation with Secrist, Dirks researched public records and spoke with those in the industry about the Secrist allegations. Most in the industry believed that Secrist had fabricated the tale. Nonetheless, on 19 March 1973, Dirks paid a visit to Equity Funding headquarters in Los Angeles and, through conversations with employees, did verify that there was fraud. Dirks passed along the information he had obtained to a *Wall Street Journal* writer and urged him to write a story. The reporter, William Blundell, initially declined to do so because the information on Equity Funding was hearsay and, if untrue, would be libelous and result in significant and perhaps irreparable damage to the company. Dirks then turned to word-of-mouth dissemination and advised clients to sell their Equity Funding stock, a move that helped them avoid the substantial losses experienced by other investors when Equity Funding went into receivership shortly thereafter.

Blundell then had a change of heart and arranged for a meeting on 27 March 1973 with the SEC and Dirks. As Dirks and Blundell met with the SEC in Los Angeles, the *Wall Street Journal* published a denial of the rumors surrounding Equity Funding. On 28 March 1973, the SEC suspended trading in the stock. On 2 April 1973, the eventual *Wall Street Journal* article by Blundell, which subsequently won a Pulitzer Prize, was published and the SEC filed a complaint against Equity Funding.[9]

As a result of the Equity Funding investigation, the SEC also investigated Dirks and the legality of his passing the information he had about Equity Funding along to his clients. Dirks had no formal relationship with any of the Delafield Childs institutional clients. He simply familiarized himself with their investment objectives and passed along information that he thought might be helpful to them. Dirks did not receive direct compensation from these clients. Rather, the clients, if they found his information valuable, would direct some of their brokerage business to Delafield Childs, a practice that earned Delafield Childs commissions. Dirks was paid a salary plus a commission by his firm, with the commission coming from his clients who directed trades through his employer.[10]

The SEC eventually censured Dirks for insider trading. His appeal of that censure, however, resulted in the U.S. Supreme Court's exoneration of Dirks and his profession with this explanation:

> It is commonplace for analysts to "ferret out and analyze information," and this often is done by meeting with and questioning corporate officers and others who are insiders. And information that the analysts obtain normally may be the basis for judgments as to the market worth of a corporation's securities. The analyst's judgment in this respect is made available in market letters or otherwise to clients of the firm. It is the nature of this type of information, and indeed of the markets themselves, that such information

[9]The stock was at $26 per share when Dirks began his investigation, and it dropped to $15 per share just prior to the public announcement of bankruptcy; see William Blundell, "A Scandal Unfolds: Some Assets Missing, Insurance Called Bogus at Equity Funding Life," *Wall Street Journal* (2 April 1973):A1.

[10]The evidence in the case did not disclose how many of the clients Dirks told about Equity Funding promised to direct brokerage business to Dirks' company as a result of his providing the critical Equity Funding information. There was at least one promise from one client of $25,000 in commissions for Dirks as a result of the Equity Funding information supplied to the client (*Dirks v. SEC* 1983).

cannot be made simultaneously available to all of the corporation's stockholders or the public generally. (*Dirks v. SEC* 1983, p. 659)

The court noted that without Dirks' efforts, the fraud might have gone on even longer and that Dirks did not benefit directly from his selective dissemination of the Equity Funding information (*Dirks v. SEC* 1983). Furthermore, the court held that because Dirks did not benefit personally from the information, and because he was not an insider, he was under no duty to abstain from trading or passing along the market-moving information. In a little-noticed portion of the case, the court also noted that Dirks was meeting directly with Equity Funding officers and was not involved in seeking or paying for tips from Equity Funding employees. This distinction would become a critical one in later insider trading cases involving fund managers, analysts, and the use of expert networks.

"The Decade of Greed" in Life and Film. In 1986, the markets had to cope with the Ivan Boesky insider trading issues and Michael Milken's junk bond offers. The cases captured the public's attention because the fictional Gordon Gekko's mantra of "Greed is good" fueled public backlash about investment markets.[11] The perception of an unfair playing field or asymmetrical dissemination of information to movers and shakers or to lucky clients by an analyst perpetuated a public unease about the profession (see Rozeff and Zaman 1988; Seyhun 1986; Zetlin 1990).

Dennis Levine, an investment banker with Drexel Burnham Lambert, was a merger specialist who used day trips to the Bahamas to phone in (from public pay phones) instructions on stock trades in advance of the public disclosure of pending mergers. Levine obtained information from a young associate at a law firm who was working on the merger documents. This young associate passed similar premerger information along to other Wall Street professionals, including Ivan Boesky (Walter 1991). Boesky paid $100 million in penalties as a result of the profits he earned from the tips he received from Levine (Frantz 1987). The charges against Levine involved 54 takeovers (corporate mergers and acquisitions). What was significant in terms of the investment and stock market culture was that Levine was not involved with clients in structuring 35 of these takeovers; his information was coming from other sources at law firms and investment banks who were handling the takeovers.[12]

Boesky's conduct stunned even his experienced defense lawyer, Harvey Pitt (Arbogast 2009). Not only was he trading on advance notice of mergers;

[11]The quote from the movie *Wall Street* (1987) was actually taken from a May 1986 commencement address Ivan Boesky gave at Berkeley in which he said, "Greed is all right. . . . Greed is healthy. You can be greedy and still feel good about yourself." As quoted in Christopher R. Brauchli, "From the Wool-Sack," *Colorado Lawyer* (August 2002):43.

[12]James B. Stewart, "Fallen Star," *Wall Street Journal* (15 May 1986):A1.

he was (together with Michael Milken) creating the corporations that were staging the takeover offers. Those corporations were funded by bonds that Milken was selling, bonds that had as their security the assets of the companies the funds raised through the bonds would be used to purchase if Milken could negotiate a deal for the takeover. This type of deal is known as a leveraged buy-out (LBO). Drexel Burnham Lambert issued statements to shareholders indicating that the firm was "highly confident" that the financing for the takeover would be in place when needed and, as a result, convinced the shareholders of the target companies to take the LBOs seriously (Ribstein 2006). Following successful takeovers, Milken became known for his "scorched earth" tactic of selling off all of the companies' assets and closing down the business. When the takeovers failed, investors were left with what came to be called "junk bonds."

Milken entered a guilty plea to six felonies and paid a $600 million fine (Stewart 1991). Drexel Burnham Lambert vigorously denied any wrongdoing but eventually pleaded guilty to six counts of fraud and paid a $300 million fine. Within months after the settlement of the criminal charges, Drexel Burnham Lambert declared bankruptcy (Simons 2002).

Prudential. Also in the 1980s came the sale of $8 billion of risky limited partnership interests by Prudential Securities. Key to the sales were the age-old representations by advisers that the investments were "safe and secure" and the lack of disclosure by the advisers of their own conflicts of interests in terms of compensation in selling the partnerships to those investors who should have been placed in lower-risk retirement investment opportunities. The advisers earned higher commissions if their clients invested in the Prudential partnerships instead of placing them in low-risk securities (Eichenwald 2005, p. 7). The sales went on for nearly a decade. Former SEC Chairman Arthur Levitt noted,

> Sadly, many people saving for retirement were misled about the risks of these investments. The SEC, with the help of state regulators, investigated and reached a settlement with Prudential . . . which has already returned almost $825 million to more than 100,000 defrauded investors.[13]

A decade later, Prudential had to settle a $410 million fine for misleading customers in the sale of insurance policies.

Regulatory Responses. Consistent with historical patterns, the public outcry in the Boesky/Milken era about the behavior of market professionals and the resulting losses caused regulatory reforms to be enacted. This era's chief reform was the Insider Trading Sanctions Act (15 U.S.C. § 78u-1, 2002),

[13]Speech to National Association of Investors Corporation, Memphis, Tennessee (27 August 1995): 1995 WL 520185.

which made it possible for the government to recover as a penalty three times the amount of profit made or loss avoided from the inside deal. The Insider Trading and Securities Fraud Enforcement Act (15 U.S.C. § 78ff, 2002) upped the penalties for insider trading to 20 years and $25,000,000. Additional penalties and more stringent jail sentences were the response to the widespread problem of market insiders using proprietary information for personal gain.

Deregulation, Savings & Loan Issues, and Reregulation. Beginning in 1980, a pattern of deregulation ran parallel to the evolving scandals of the decade. The passage of the Depository Institutions Deregulation and Monetary Control Act (12 U.S.C. §226, 1980) allowed the setup of the next wave of fraud and abuse in a different market segment. The act gave savings and loan (S&L) associations expanded abilities in terms of the nature of their loans and the right to offer savings products beyond the basic deposit account. The events that followed this deregulation illustrate how swings from regulation to deregulation remind us of the reasons for the original regulation.

Lincoln Savings & Loan became the poster child for the lack of wisdom in the deregulation of the S&Ls. Like its counterparts in the stock market, Lincoln's ultimate collapse began with advisers steering depositors into noninsured and highly speculative investments that were actually not in the Lincoln Savings & Loan but in American Continental Corporation (ACC), a real estate development company owned by Charles Keating. ACC had purchased Lincoln. The depositors who were steered into the ACC investments were elderly, unsophisticated, and dependent on their investments for their retirement incomes. In 1988, the real estate bubble of that era burst, and in 1989, Lincoln Savings and Loan collapsed, at a cost of more than $3 billion to the federal government. Some 23,000 Lincoln bondholders had been defrauded, and many investors lost their life savings. The depositors who held land investments through ACC lost everything. The limited deposits they had in Lincoln were insured by the federal government, and the government had to reimburse them for those losses, but their ACC holdings were not insured and not reimbursed.

The political fallout was extensive because three U.S. senators received campaign contributions from Keating in exchange for the senators' help with regulators in connection with Lincoln's situation. The result of this intervention was that the regulatory scrutiny of Lincoln ceased (Dillon and Cannon 2010).

The end of the real estate bubble affected other S&Ls that had, in the euphoria of their new deregulated business model, made loans without appraisals or income verification—a theme that would reemerge 15 years later in another, larger real estate bubble. The fallout from the market collapse of 1988–1989 was the closing or other resolution (acquisition or merger) by the federal government of 1,043 S&Ls that held $519 billion in assets. A total of almost 4,000 bankers from the S&L collapses were sent to prison for various financial fraud crimes (Tett 2009).

When all of the depositor/investor cases related to Lincoln and American Continental and the other S&Ls made their way into federal court, Judge Stanley Sporkin asked the questions that summarized in a nutshell the events of the 1980s and early 1990s, questions that we have repeated in the decades to follow as new scandals unfolded:

> Where were these professionals, a number of whom are now asserting their rights under the Fifth Amendment, when these clearly improper transactions were being consummated? Why didn't any of them speak up or disassociate themselves from the transactions? Where also were the outside accountants and attorneys when these transactions were effectuated? What is difficult to understand is that with all the professional talent involved (both accounting and legal), why at least one professional would not have blown the whistle to stop the overreaching that took place in this case.[14]

Judge Sporkin's basic question, where was everybody, would be repeated as additional ethical and legal issues emerged over the next three decades (Jennings 2003).

The regulation that resulted from the collapse of the S&L system was the Financial Institutions Reform, Recovery and Enforcement Act of 1989, which specified new minimum capital requirements for loans and restricted the types of assets that S&Ls could hold (12 U.S.C. § 191 et seq). Additional regulation of appraisal and appraisers and the setting of loan-writing standards resulted at both the state and federal levels.

By the end of the 1980s, public perception of investment markets had reached a new low because of these incidents and also because Hollywood's depiction of the professionals involved in those incidents, as in the film *Wall Street* (1987), became legendary (Padilla 2008). In a *Wall Street Journal* poll, 76% of the respondents who invested in stock markets indicated that they believed insider trading among Wall Street professionals was common and 69% of all adults surveyed believed it was a common practice. Public perception is formulated by the culture and "that perception accompanies voters to the ballot box and jury boxes" (Ribstein 2006, p. 200). And it is a factor that influences public policy and regulation.

The Dark Decade

During the decade that ran from 1991 to 2001, ethical contentions continued over soft dollars, but much more to grapple with arose as the dot-com bubble burst. And the rise and fall of Enron occurred in less than 10 years.

[14]*Lincoln Savings & Loan Association vs. Wall*, 743 F. Sup: 901, 920 (D.D.C. 1989).

Soft Dollars and Analyst Issues Going into the Dot-Com Bubble. By the 1990s, the predominant Wall Street business model for delivering research was soft dollar pricing, which provided fund managers with research produced by analyst employees at the full-service brokerage firms (investment banking firms). Throughout the 1990s, these soft dollar arrangements went largely undisclosed and/or misunderstood by fund beneficiaries, even as academics, the media, and regulators were raising questions about the lack of transparency, the real cost, and the independence of the research being furnished through these arrangements.

The well-concealed interrelationships in soft dollar arrangements soon became a topic of regular business press coverage. Analyses pointed out the effects of the conflicts of interests that resulted from the loyalties and incentives of analysts providing the research. A so-called Chinese wall (also called a "firewall") of separation between the analyst/research side of the brokerage house and the investment banking and trading side of the house was touted as a solution for avoiding such conflicts of interests. In practice, however, the independence was compromised.

In 1992, the *Wall Street Journal,* reporting on the realities of investment banking operations, indicated that no firewalls were in effect. Some investment analysts were told to avoid negative statements about clients of the firm (Siconolfi 1992). In addition, some analysts were expected to do more than simply offer favorable ratings. They were told to "pound the table" to sell the stocks that they had rated favorably (Dorfman 1997).

As the popular business press continued its investigative reporting on actual analyst practices, academic studies were under way that eventually reached the same conclusion as the media: Analysts who were employees of brokerage houses (investment bankers) had inherent biases (Lin and McNichols 1998). One of the biases was a reluctance to downgrade stocks, particularly those stocks of companies that were clients of the analysts' firms. Independent analysts had very different recommendations from those of analysts who worked for brokerage firms that were lead or co-lead underwriters for stock offerings (Michaely and Womack 1999). The following summary indicates the quantitative level of influence that firm underwriting had on the firm's research analysts: During the February 1996–June 2003 period, the average daily abnormal return to independent research firm "buy" recommendations exceeded that of the investment banks by 3.1 bps, or almost 8 percentage points annualized (Barber, Lehavy, and Trueman 2007). In contrast, during this period, those investment bank "buy" recommendations subsequent to equity offerings underperformed those of independent research firms by 8.7 bps (almost 22% annualized). The underperformance of investment bank buy recommendations was found to be a reluctance among employee analysts to downgrade stocks that should have been downgraded (Barber, Lehavy, and Trueman 2007).

Once the research on the macro effects of analysts' conflicts percolated out of academia, the business press began delving into analyst practices and was able to document bias through the data. For example, in 1998, the *Wall Street Journal* reviewed 2,066 analysts' recommendations and found that 68% of the analyst recommendations were "strong buys" or "buys," 31% were "holds," and fewer than 1% were "sells."[15]

Other studies concluded that another systemic problem was that analysts are overly optimistic, something attributed to the influence of the "sales" side of the firms and the sales side (i.e., investment bankers) being the analysts' source of income; analysts' work was evaluated within the context of the underwriters' ability to generate revenue (Bailey and Syre 1996).

Regulation Full Disclosure. In 2000, the SEC adopted Regulation Full Disclosure, or Regulation FD (17 C.F.R. § 243). It was a long time in the making and was intended to curb and clarify the responsibilities of analysts who obtain material nonpublic information. The rule was that the analysts had to make public any material nonpublic information that they obtained from company insiders. The earnings conference call was born as a result of this rule. Company information was released in a preannounced (and potentially international) telephone conference call so that the same information was disclosed to all participating parties. Whatever information companies disclosed was then almost instantly available via the internet.

Interestingly, and perhaps presciently, credit rating analysts were exempt from the full disclosure requirements of Regulation FD because, the commission noted, the credit rating agencies were performing a public service and not subject to the same pressures as other analysts who might be tempted to use the information for personal or firm gain (Evans 2012). Although Regulation FD seems fairly straightforward, its clarity did not deter some analysts from developing alternative methods for obtaining material nonpublic information. Those efforts would emerge in the context of criminal insider trading cases against analysts for their "expert networks."

Enron and Analyst Issues. Enron Corporation, a natural gas company that became an energy trading company, was built during the dot-com era, and its fall became a symbol of the era's end. The problems with Enron's accounting went largely unnoticed and/or undocumented by analysts. The conflicts of interests analysts faced were extremely damaging to their objectivity and, eventually, their firms' clients (Macey 2004). In fact, those who

[15]John Hechinger, "Heard in New England: Analysts May Hate to Say 'Sell,' But a Few Companies Do Hear It," *Wall Street Journal* (8 April 1998):B2.

raised questions about the company or suggested a "sell" recommendation for it were banished from their jobs. For example, Chung Wu was an investment bank analyst employed by UBS Paine Webber. In the summer of 2001, when he recommended that his clients sell their Enron stock, he was fired.[16] UBS Paine Webber administered the Enron employee stock option plan, so the firm continued with its "strong buy" position even after terminating Wu. The price of Enron shares on the day of Wu's termination was $36. Within three months of the date of Wu's termination, Enron declared bankruptcy and its stock was trading at $0.61 per share. It later became completely worthless.

Wu's firing came from a recommendation made close to the time of Enron's collapse. A few analysts, however, were raising questions at a time when corrective action might have been taken. During the 1990s, John Olson, an analyst with Merrill Lynch, was cautioning his clients about Enron.[17] In 2001, he issued a firm "sell" recommendation on Enron, and when Enron executives read Olson's recommendation, Ken Lay, who was then chairman of Enron, wrote a letter to Olson's employer saying, "John Olson has been wrong about Enron for more than 10 years and is still wrong. [B]ut he is consistant [sic]."[18] Olson was fired.

Wu and Olson were loners who were fired for their correct analyses and advice on a company that was engaged in fraud. Just how alone they were indicates a lapse among analysts in terms of candid evaluations of securities and companies. In October 2001, with Enron's share price at half of its previous high just six months earlier and with numerous business press articles raising serious questions about Enron's Byzantine financial structure and statements, 16 of Thomson Financial/First Call's analysts rated Enron a "buy" and 13 of those analysts called it a "strong buy." Even after the November SEC disclosure of its investigation of Enron, 11 of the 13 analysts continued with their "strong buy" recommendations. Only one "sell" recommendation came from the group of 29 analysts, yet Enron was less than a month away from bankruptcy (Hill 2002). The director of research for Thomson Financial testified at the hearing before the U.S. Senate Committee on Governmental Affairs on Enron's collapse as follows:

---

[16]Richard A. Oppel, Jr., "The Man Who Paid for Sizing Up Enron," *New York Times* (27 March 2002):C1.

[17]Permanent Subcommittee on Investigations, "The Role of the Board of Directors in Enron's Collapse," S. Re: No. 107-70 (2002):39–40.

[18]John Schwartz, "Enron's Collapse: The Analyst; Man Who Doubted Enron Enjoys New Recognition," *New York Times* (21 January 2002):C8. Olson explained that when his boss showed him the note from Lay, he responded, "[Y]ou know that I'm old and worthless, but at least I can spell 'consistent.'" Olson's wry observation after being terminated was that too many Wall Street analysts in search of fame and glory are "schnuckels," a Yiddish word for dupes.

> By November 12, almost a month after Enron had announced a $1.2 billion write-off that Ken Lay could not explain on a conference call, almost a month after the *Wall Street Journal* reported Enron executives stood to make millions from Enron partnerships, [three] weeks after the CFO was fired, [two] weeks after Enron announced it was being investigated by the SEC, and [four] days after Enron announced that it had overstated [four] years of earnings by $600 million . . . there were still eight analysts with a strong buy, three with a buy, one with a hold, and one with a strong sell. At that point, none had dropped their recommendations. (Hill 2002, p. 54–55)

The Dot-Com Bubble. The dot-com bubble in the making followed a path similar to that of Enron, with great demand for the companies' stocks and admiration of company managers.

This bubble was similar to the railroad trust bubble of the 1920s, in that investors were not clear about the true risk involved in the rapid rounds of IPOs. Prior to the dot-com era, standard underwriting practice required that a company show three years of profitability before being taken public. In the dot-com craze, those profitability requirements were lessened to the point of being nonexistent.

Also similar to the 1920s market structure was the practice of prearranged market demand for the dot-com shares, referred to by the SEC as "spinning." Shares in an IPO were allocated to favored clients in exchange for their promises that they would jump in and buy more shares in the IPO but at a price higher than that which the underwriter had established for the IPO. In effect, an IPO was "price-structured" before it began; buyers had already been locked in at prices higher than the initial price when the offering was made. As in the 1920s investment trusts, the demand and prices were synthetic. The gatekeepers, those who were charged with supervision of market offerings, were unwilling, however, to point out the true financial conditions of the start-up companies or disclose the positions of the underwriters (Coffee 2002). The asymmetrical information problem that led to the first federal regulations of the securities market remained a problem in the dot-com era.

The confidence inspired by rapid changes in technology resulted in IPOs and secondary stock offerings of companies that turned out to be nothing more substantial than the frauds that spawned the Kansas blue sky regulations in 1911. There was, however, an additional issue that would emerge after the dot-com bubble burst. That issue involved the same conflict that the Pecora hearing uncovered: Analysts were saying one thing publicly, but their knowledge and internal communications reflected a different view.

As the bubble grew, the IPOs continued to carry the blessing of favorable ratings from analysts housed at the investment banking firms that were leading the IPOs. Like so many of the markets in this historical review, the dot-com era was another bull market during which stock prices, together with the enthusiasm of analysts for the affected stocks, seemed to know no upper limit. The accuracy of those ratings can be judged in hindsight by the markets' collapses. The most troubling aspect of the situation, however, is that analysts had knowledge of the inaccuracy of the ratings and recommendations in real time but did not act on that knowledge—a reflection of the underlying conflicts of interests (Francis, Chen, Philbrick, and Willis 2004).

The positive analysts' recommendations for companies and securities that would end in bankruptcy often resulted from close relationships with the companies themselves (Jennings 2003). Employee analysts producing research for their firms sang the praises of their brokers' stocks. In a 1999 speech to the Securities Industry Association in Boca Raton, Florida, Arthur Levitt, who was then chairman of the SEC, publicly expressed concern about the role of analysts in touting stocks their firms were offering and about the "unspoken pressures" they were facing to report that "what looks like a frog is really a prince."[19] The speech included the following assessment:

> I worry that investors are being influenced too much by analysts whose evaluations read like they graduated from the Lake Wobegone School of Securities Analysis—the one that boasts that all its securities are above average. And I worry that investors hear from too many analysts who—whether they realize it or not—may be just a bit too eager to report that what looks like a frog is really a prince. Well, that's just not the way it is: Every investor and every analyst must beware that—to paraphrase a very different type of analyst—sometimes a frog is just a frog.[20]

In the 1980s, the ratio of analysts' recommendations to "buy" versus "sell" was one to one. By the time of Levitt's public comments, the ratio was 1% "sell" to 68% "buy" (Hong and Kubik 2003). The *Wall Street Journal* warned that "the analyst is wearing two hats" and that investment banks

> have persuaded clients to hire underwriters on the basis of their analysts' selling power . . . [and] in turn, the analyst's worth is increasingly dependent on his or her ability to bring in deals.[21]

The *Boston Globe* had a stinging warning: "Trust analysts at your peril."[22]

[19]"Frog Spawn," *Economist* (15 April 1999): http://www.economist.com/node/321068.

[20]Arthur Levitt, "Remarks before the Securities Industry Association's Legal and Compliance Seminar," SEC Chairman's Speech, Boca Raton, FL (13 April 1999): http://www.sec.gov/news/speech/speecharchive/1999/spch266.htm.

[21]Roger Lowenstein, "Today's Analyst Often Wears Two Hats," *Wall Street Journal* (2 May 1996):A1.

[22]Steve Baily and Steven Syre, "Taking Analysts' Tempting Forecasts with Grain of Salt," *Boston Globe* (23 October 1996):C1.

The *Globe* could have been thinking of Henry Blodget, a Merrill Lynch internet star analyst who touted shares to the public that he privately referred to in e-mails as "junk," "a piece of junk," or "a piece of [expletive]."[23]

Salomon Smith Barney was scrutinized for its relationship with WorldCom. The investment firm's employees were so intertwined with the company that they attended WorldCom board meetings and offered ideas. At the same time, the analysts continued to issue the company their highest ratings, despite knowledge of WorldCom's debt levels and accounting issues that ultimately caused the company's demise.[24] Jack Grubman, known as a superstar analyst for Salomon Smith Barney, said, right before the company's collapse in 2002, "If one were to find the comparables to WorldCom . . . [t]he list would be very short and would include the likes of Merck, Home Depot, Wal-Mart, Coke, Microsoft, Gillette, and Disney."[25] (The parent company of Salomon Smith Barney was Citigroup, which served as the investment banker for WorldCom and which also gave a half a billion dollars in loans to WorldCom's CEO, Bernard Ebbers.) Grubman made a public recommendation of "buy" for WorldCom, which he described in an e-mail to two colleagues as a "pig."

The interrelationships were documented by the analysts' own words. Their private e-mails became public, and their private statements contradicted their recommendations on companies and securities. Grubman's e-mails were particularly damaging for the integrity of analysts. Sanford Weill, the former CEO of Citigroup, leaned on Grubman for a favorable rating of AT&T, a company whose chairman's support he was seeking in an internal Citigroup power struggle, in exchange for Weill's influence in getting Grubman's twins into a high-class Manhattan preschool.[26]

Following Grubman's upgraded rating, C. Michael Armstrong, who was then CEO of AT&T, sided with Weill in the battle for control of Citigroup against Citigroup's co-CEO, John Reed. The New York Attorney General declined to prosecute anyone involved in this situation. The practice of an analyst changing a recommendation for personal advantage, however, raises ethical issues beyond the general conflicts in the relationships between analysts and their investment bank employers.

---

[23]*Merrill Lynch & Co.*, 273 (S.D.N.Y. 2003), F. Supp. 2d 351:381.

[24]Andrew Backover and Jayne O'Donnell, "WorldCom Scrutiny Touches on E-Mail," *USA Today* (8 July 2002):1B.

[25]Posted on WorldCom's website up through 7 August 2002.

[26]Mara Der Hovanasian, "Can Citi Regroup?" *BusinessWeek* (9 November 2007):31. The history is found in Charles Gasparino, "Ghosts of E-Mails Continue to Haunt Wall Street," *Wall Street Journal* (18 November 2002):C1, C13, and Charles Gasparino, Anita Raghavan, and Rebecca Blumenstein, "Citigroup Now Has New Worry: What Grubman Will Say," *Wall Street Journal* (10 October 2002):A1.

Incidents such as these, and the ongoing collapses among the dot-coms, resulted in a great deal of unfavorable business press. The cover of *Fortune* on 14 May 2001, just after the dot-com bubble burst, featured analyst Mary Meeker, a Wall Street analyst well connected to the Silicon Valley start-ups, and the caption, "Can We Ever Trust Again?"

Still, one year later, *Fortune* suggested that at least some analysts could be trusted. The magazine featured Sallie Krawcheck and the caption, "In Search of the Last Honest Analyst," on the cover of the 10 June 2002 issue. And beneath the caption was the telling phrase, "Her analysts are paid for research, not deals." This issue was published after Enron and WorldCom had collapsed and Dennis Kozlowski had been charged with embezzlement at Tyco, the company where he served as CEO.

The reputational damage to the profession was wide and deep.[27] In 2002, CBS News conducted a poll regarding the American people's confidence in big business. The poll was conducted among a nationwide random sample of 685 adults. The results showed that 68% believed that insider trading was a widespread practice (Padilla 2008). CBS was measuring an old issue (from the Boesky era), but the perception of the public was the same because of all the market events at the time and resulting disclosure about the behavior of investment professionals.

Furthermore, the literature indicated that the problems of previous markets had not been solved and were writ large in this era. John Coffee cautioned about the root causes:

> But the starting point for an intelligent debate is the recognition that the two major, contemporary crises now facing the securities markets (i.e., the collapse of Enron and the growing controversy over securities analysts) which began with the New York Attorney General's investigation into

[27]In addition to the press reports already cited, see Jeffrey Laderman, "Who Can You Trust?" *BusinessWeek* (5 October 1998): "Brokerage firms are not about to break up the money machine that pairs analysts with dealmakers. And analysts are not about to risk offending the companies they cover. Woe to the investor who doesn't keep these two ideas in mind before investing on a stock recommendation" (p. 156); SEC Chairman Arthur Levitt, Address at the Investors' Town Meeting, Albuquerque, New Mexico (20 November 1999): "Analysts' paychecks are typically tied to the performance of their employers. You can imagine how unpopular an analyst would be who downgrades his firm's best client. Is it any wonder that today, a 'sell' recommendation from an analyst is as common as a Barbara Streisand concert?"; Erick Schonfeld, "The High Price of Research," *Fortune* (20 March 2000): "Analysts of all stripes . . . increasingly derive a portion of their compensation, directly or indirectly, from the companies they cover."; Robert Samuelson, *Newsweek* (3 April 2000), quoting Jay Ritter as stating, "The conflicts of interest are immense" and that stock analysts are increasingly "cheerleaders" whose pay depends on the firm's underwriting, which depends on enthusiastic research reports; Eileen Buckley, "Holding Analysts Accountable," *Industry Standard* (12 June 2000): "Research analysts writing recommendations of closely watched Internet stocks routinely face conflicts of interest."

> Merrill, Lynch, involve at bottom the same problem—both are crises motivated by the discovery by investors that reputational intermediaries upon whom they relied were conflicted and seemingly sold their interests short. Neither the law nor the market has yet solved either of these closely related problems. (Coffee 2002, p. 1420)

Eliot Spitzer, the Global Settlement, and SEC Changes. Determined to address the conflicts that Coffee identified, the SEC conducted a study and then sent a report to Congress in 2001 entitled "Analyzing the Analysts: Are Investors Getting Unbiased Research from Wall Street?" The report contained these conclusions:

- It was commonplace for research analysts to provide research reports on companies that the analysts' employer firm underwrote.
- Many firms paid their analysts largely based on the profitability of the firms' investment banking units.
- Investment bankers at some firms were involved in evaluating the firm's research analysts to determine their compensation.
- Some firms maintained policies prohibiting analysts from owning stock in companies they covered. Other firms permitted analysts to own stock in companies they covered but prohibited them from executing personal trades that were contrary to the analysts' outstanding recommendations.
- Compliance with SRO rules that require firms to monitor the private equity investments of employees, including analysts, was poor. Firms did not always know whether their research analysts owned stock in companies about which their analysts issued research reports.[28]

As a result of the report, the SEC worked with both the NYSE and NASD to address the conflicts of interests. After the regulatory process obtained public comments on the findings and the proposed changes from the SROs and the SEC, the following changes were made:

- Analyst compensation could not be tied to specific investment banking transactions.
- Analysts' personal trading in securities of companies they were following for their companies was restricted.
- Analysts could not offer favorable research in exchange for business for their firms.

[28]The report is available at http://fcic-static.law.stanford.edu/cdn_media/fcic-docs/2003-05-07%20William%20H.%20Donaldson%20Testimony%20Concerning%20Global%20Research%20Analyst%20Settlement.pdf.

- Investment banking review of analysts' research reports was restricted.
- There would be quiet periods for the issuance of research reports of 40 days by analysts on IPOs if their firms had worked on the IPO.[29]

Running parallel with the congressional and SEC actions were the civil suit that New York Attorney General Eliot Spitzer filed against Merrill Lynch & Co. and Henry M. Blodget as well as numbers of investor suits. In May 2003, the SEC and Spitzer's office, together with the NYSE and NASD, reached what became known as the "global settlement" for the civil charges and all the individual suits that had been filed against the analysts and their firms for misleading recommendations on the dot-com stocks. Merrill Lynch settled its case with Spitzer separately for $100 million and agreed to certain structural changes and policies to prevent the conflicts that created the inconsistencies between research findings and public recommendations from which Blodget's work suffered. The other investment banking firms agreed to pay $875 million into a fund to be used to benefit customers who had lost money by following the analysts' public recommendations. The civil penalties paid in addition by the firms totaled $487.5 million, with the penalties distributed jointly and severally among the firms.[30]

Two additional monetary components of the settlement were designed to address issues that could help investors in the future. The first required the firms to pay $432.5 million over a five-year period for the purchase of independent third-party research. The firms were required to notify customers on their account statements of the availability of the independent research for purposes of evaluating their portfolios. The second requirement was $80 million for an Investor Education Fund.

The settlement marked the end of specific cases, but its terms required that it be only the beginning of additional reforms. For example, three months later, the SEC issued Regulation Analyst Certification, a rule that requires analysts to certify that their research reports accurately reflect their personal views.

[29]This 2003 rule was eliminated by the JOBS (Jumpstart Our Business Startups) Act of 2012. The JOBS Act applies to corporations with less than $1 billion in annual revenue and allows analysts' reports (analysts whose firms have worked on the IPO) to be published immediately. Wall Street has followed a 25-day quiet period anyway, however, for IPOs issued after JOBS. The reason for the voluntary quiet period was the fear that the provision in the act would be challenged. The 40-day rule was a settlement negotiated by Eliot Spitzer, and the federal government was overriding it with JOBS, something lawyers were unclear about in terms of states' rights, preemption, and a host of other legal confusions the JOBS created.

[30]In individual settlements, Henry Blodget was required to pay a $2 million fine and Jack Grubman paid a $7.5 million fine (related to his recommendation on Winstar); neither of them admitted or denied the charges.

Reliance on Financial Statements: Sarbanes–Oxley Reforms. At the same time the regulatory reforms for analysts were being developed, the Sarbanes–Oxley Act (SOX) was enacted.[31] SOX includes regulatory reforms for corporate officers and directors and for external auditors. Because financial analysis is only as good as the integrity of the financial reports on which it is based, the SOX reforms were directed at improving the quality of company financial reporting through structural changes in corporate governance, auditor relationships with clients, and increased penalties for false financial statements. Included in the structural changes were increased requirements for certification of internal controls. Although the SOX reforms were not directed at analysts, they did address the same basic ethical issues analysts have faced, such as conflicts of interests and the question of whether what auditors say in their certifications about the solvency of companies correctly reflects their personal views.

Ironically, SOX may have created a false sense of security about financial statements. Because the federal government assumed a role in overseeing the accounting profession and mandatory rule changes resulted, some investors made questionable assumptions about accounting and financial reporting standards. For example, they assumed that the loophole that permitted Enron to spin debt off its books through the special purposes entity (SPE) exception for financial statement consolidation had been closed. The rule was changed, but as later market collapses would show, the loophole was not closed. A recurring theme in financial markets is, "It takes FASB two years to issue a ruling and the investment bankers two weeks to figure out a way around it."[32] Fewer than five years passed before another market bubble burst upon the discovery that the financial statements of collapsed firms may have been certified as true but remained misleading.

The Real Estate/Mortgage Bubble

As the debate over conflicts continued and the technology market continued growing, the second phase of deregulation (uninformed by the S&L experience) began. This change would fuel the mortgage/real estate bubble of a decade later. In 1993, the Secretary of the Treasury, Robert Rubin, together with congressional allies, worked to repeal Glass–Steagall and thereby remove the wall that had been set up between commercial and investment banking (Freeman 2010).[33] The immediate result was the merger of Citigroup and Traveler's

[31]The Sarbanes–Oxley Act of 2002 is Pub. L. No. 107-204, §§ 902-06, 116 Stat. 745, 805-06 (codified throughout sections in 18 and 28 U.S.C. [2006]).

[32]Mark P. Holtzman, Elizabeth Venuti, and Robert Fonfeder, quoting Richard Leftwich, in "Enron and the Raptors: SPEs That Flourish in Loopholes," *CPA Journal* (8 June 2003), p. 7.

[33]Glass–Steagall was repealed by the Gramm-Leach-Bliley Financial Modernization Act, P.L. 106–102 (12 November 1999).

Insurance without the divestitures that Glass–Steagall would have required. For the first time since the post-1929 legislation, the federal government was scaling back its Wall Street supervision and trusting the unregulated market to organize the economy according to free and open trade.[34]

Once the division of commercial and investment banking was eliminated, the character and structure of investment banking firms changed, as did the size and nature of the U.S. mortgage market. Between 1990 and 2001, home mortgage debt doubled. Between 2001 and 2006, home mortgage debt doubled again.[35] The intriguing part of the second doubling was that 60% of the mortgages issued during the 2001–2006 era were adjustable rate mortgages, and payments due from borrowers generally increased after two to three years at the low rate (Murdock 2011). In addition, the dollar amount of low-to-moderate-income loans or subprime loans increased to 25% of total mortgage investment dollars. A 1600% increase occurred in Alt-A loans (i.e., Alternative A-paper, also known as "liar's loans"). These loans typically are not backed by the income documentation required for traditional underwriting (Murdock 2011). By 2006, when the interest rate adjustments began to take effect, the default rate on these new forms of mortgage increased from a range of 4%–8% to one of 22%–37% (Federal Reserve Data 2004–2009).

More than 75% of the subprime mortgages that were originated in the first quarter of 2007 had been bundled and sold as mortgage-backed securities (MBS). With an accompanying increase in the availability of investment dollars worldwide, an expanded mortgage market, and climbing real estate prices, investment bankers seized the moment to create various pools of purchased mortgages to sell as MBS. Reminiscent of the railroad boom, the MBS market, based on real estate sales, increased in dollar amount by 135% from 2000 to 2007. As this market grew, so also did the compensation for those who were putting together all the securitized offerings. The average Wall Street bonus increased from $74,140 in 2001 to $99,930 in 2003, but between 2003 and 2006, it almost doubled—to $190,600.[36] As history has demonstrated, many believed that the market and real estate values would increase *ad infinitum* (Dennis 2009).

---

[34]Alan Greenspan, then-chairman of the Federal Reserve, testified before Congress on 7 April 2010 that he had favored the scale-back of federal regulation of the market, but realized that following the 2008 financial collapse that he was wrong about the need for regulation. His testimony can be found at http://www.c-spanvideo.org/program/292886-1.

[35]Board of Governors of the Federal Reserve System, Federal Reserve Statistical Release Z.1, Flow of Funds Accounts of the United States, 8, 59 (2008): http://www.federalreserve.gov/releases/z1/20080306/.

[36]Press Release, Office of the State Deputy Comptroller, New York City Sec. Indus. Bonuses (28 January 2009): http://www.osc.state.ny.us/press/releases/jan08/bonus.pdf.

The result of the growth in the number of mortgages, the lower lending standards, and the securitization of mortgage debt was that the truth about the value of the mortgages and the collateral (houses) was publicly unknown. So, when the credit rating agencies downgraded a small segment of MBS, marketwide concerns erupted and a sell-off began. The financial losses for U.S. institutions in 2008 totaled $3.6 trillion.[37] The cover story of *Fortune* magazine for 26 November 2009 was titled "What Were They Smoking?" and indicted those who headed the investment firms fueling the run-up.[38] The cover featured those words in a 3.5-inch headline with photographs of Charles Prince of Citigroup ($9.8 billion loss), James Cayne of Bear Stearns ($450 million loss),[39] John Mack of Morgan Stanley ($3.7 billion loss), and Stanley O'Neal of Merrill Lynch ($7.9 billion loss).

The Sellers: How Did They Do It for So Long? For the purpose of this history of ethics in financial markets, the crash of 2008 brings to the fore the same critical question that arose following the end of market bubbles in the other eras: How was so much that was so obvious neither discussed nor disclosed for so long? The simple answer is that many people, particularly analysts, were aware of the problems but their concerns were limited to their private thoughts and not disclosed publicly. In fact, the documentation of concerns among analysts and others involved in the sale and evaluation of these securities during this latest era was greater than the documentation found from previous financial collapses, including even the recent Enron and dot-com eras. Again, the private reflections of analysts and managers were not consistent with the sunny outlooks they offered publicly on their MBS. For example, Ralph R. Cioffi and Matthew M. Tannin were long-term, respected managers at Bear Stearns who were responsible for a $1.6 billion hedge fund that lost 100% of its value in 2008. In April 2007, when some investors in the funds were trying to pull out as the market began to rumble, Tannin reflected his concerns as follows in an e-mail to Cioffi:

> [T]he subprime market looks pretty damn ugly. . . . If we believe [our internal modeling] is ANYWHERE CLOSE to accurate I think we should close the funds now. The reason for this is that if [our internal modeling] is correct then the entire subprime market is toast. . . . If AAA bonds are systematically downgraded then there is simply no way for us to make money—ever.[40]

[37]Henry Meyer and Ayesha Daya, "Roubini Predicts U.S. Losses May Reach $3.6 Trillion," Bloomberg (20 January 2009).

[38]"What Were They Smoking?" *Fortune* (26 November 2007). The losses in this paragraph were those depicted on the cover at that time. The losses were obviously greater than originally reported.

[39]Jennifer Levitz and Kate Kelly, "Bear Faces First Loss, Fraud Complaint," *Wall Street Journal* (15 November 2007):C1, C2.

[40]The e-mail is quoted in the indictment against the two men and can be found at http://www.justice.gov/usao/nye/pr/2008/2008jun19.html.

Tannin did not send the e-mail on the Bear Stearns system but, rather, through his private e-mail. And he sent the message to Cioffi at home, via his wife's e-mail account. That night, Tannin, Cioffi, and another colleague from Bear Stearns met at the Cioffi home to discuss the issues Tannin raised in the e-mail. Tannin left confident enough to participate in an investor call that was held two days later. He actually brought in more investors to the funds, and Cioffi told existing investors that he had invested even more of his own money into the fund, although he had not (Jennings 2008). When investors began to make calls on the funds, the two managers made heroic efforts to try and meet the cash demands, but they failed. The funds were worthless, and Bear Stearns shares, worth $171 in January 2007, were down to $10 by March 2008 (Jennings 2010b).

The experience of these two Wall Street managers is a classic case study in ethics. (Their actions did not constitute a criminal act; both men were acquitted of the securities fraud charges brought against them.) The ethical issue was the one that runs through the centuries of financial market deceptions and bubbles: Were the managers fair, truthful, and forthright with their clients and other investors in the information they disclosed about the fund? No, their private concerns were not shared publicly with their clients. In addition, these managers used the defense of "it was not a crime," thereby substituting legalistic reasoning for ethical behavior in defining the standard of duty to clients. Interestingly, however, the end result of all the misbehavior in the market eras described in this essay has been increased regulation, including the definition of new crimes and criminal penalties.

The Underwriters: How Did They Hide It for So Long? The SPE structure, pioneered by Enron, re-emerged in the real estate bubble, and Lehman Brothers was an investment firm that used SPEs to disguise its level of leverage. What has become known as the "Repo 105 maneuver" allowed Lehman to sell off its securitized instruments for cash, which was then used to pay down Lehman's debts, a practice that was particularly beneficial for the firm because pay-downs before the release of quarterly results make for phenomenal debt/equity ratios. The publicly reported ratios, in turn, allowed Lehman to continue with even greater leverage that was unknown to the investors. It was all a sleight of hand (Jennings 2011a).

Once the quarterly financials were made public, Lehman would buy back the instruments with what was referred to internally as a "5% haircut," which meant that Lehman was buying these assets back at 105% of the sale price. What Lehman was doing and how it was doing it could all be figured out through a careful study of the company's financial reports. Some advanced detective work was needed, however, to decipher what was really happening.

Lehman's actions present a classic ethical issue of something that was legal, sort of. The "shipping" of the instruments off the books had to be a sales transaction, something that had to be established through a bona fide legal opinion. No lawyer in the United States was willing to offer his or her imprimatur for these types of "shipping-through" transactions (i.e., transactions in which securities are sold for temporary purposes and then purchased back once the need for "off the books" is met). In fact, the bankruptcy trustees' report offers excerpts from interviews with several Lehman employees who said that Lehman was unable to obtain a true sale opinion from a law firm based in the United States related to the Repo 105 transactions.[41] Lehman's legal opinion on these spin-offs being sales came from the United Kingdom.

In short, the Repo 105 transactions were legally gray and ethically unfair. Within Lehman, the employees and officers were aware of the fine line they were walking as they faced increasing inquiries. One manager wrote in an e-mail about the leverage issue, "My head will explode if we have to talk to [analysts] about this again."[42] Analysts raised the questions, but never quite took their concerns to the level of confrontation, public disclosure, or regulatory reporting.

The Credit Analysts. A new regulatory target emerged from the real estate bubble and the 2008 market collapse—the credit rating analysts. The final report on the 2008 financial crisis by the Financial Crisis Inquiry Commission concluded,

> The three credit rating agencies were key enablers of the financial meltdown. The mortgage-related securities at the heart of the crisis could not have been marketed and sold without their seal of approval.[43]

From 2004 to 2007, rating agencies Moody's Investors Service and Standard & Poor's (S&P) issued investment-grade ratings for the majority of the MBS that were issued in the United States, roughly \$2.5 trillion in residential MBS (RMBS) and \$1.4 trillion in collateralized debt obligations (CDOs).[44] The ratings on these securities made up one-half of Moody's business. With the demand so great for ratings and compensation for supervisors in the firms tied to new business, the element of conflicts once again made its way into the root causes of a bubble. Credit analysts also faced the same

[41]"Trustee's Report," Chapter 11, Case No. 08-13555, p. 68.

[42]Lehman Brothers Holdings, p. 124.

[43]Financial Crisis Inquiry Commission, "The Financial Crisis Inquiry Report: Final Report of the National Commission on the Causes of the Financial and Economic Crisis in the United States" (2011), p.

[44]Staff of Senate Permanent Subcommittee on Investigations, 112th Congress, "Wall Street and the Financial Crisis: Anatomy of a Financial Collapse," Majority and Minority Staff Report 257 (Comm. Print 2011) [hereafter, "Anatomy of a Financial Collapse"], p. 8.

inherent conflicts as other analysts related to who is paying. The SEC report on the role of credit analysts in the 2008 market collapse concluded:

> As the Commission noted in its recent release, some observers have indicated that while conflicts of interest due to the "issuer pays" model exist with respect to all asset classes that receive ratings, the conflicts created from the "issuer pays" model in rating structured finance products, particularly RMBS and related CDOs, may be exacerbated for a number of reasons. First, the arranger is often the primary designer of the deal and as such, has more flexibility to adjust the deal structure to obtain a desired credit rating as compared to arrangers of non-structured asset classes. As well, arrangers that underwrite RMBS and CDO offerings have substantial influence over the choice of rating agencies hired to rate the deals. (SEC 2008, p. 31)

An analyst from Moody's indicated that they talked about everything in issuing their ratings "except the elephant sitting on the table." The "elephant" referred to the fact that they did not have information on the mortgages underlying the securities and that analysts were not accounting for the changes in underwriting standards for those mortgages.[45]

The congressional hearings furnished the damaging e-mails that have become a pattern in bubbles and in establishing foreknowledge on the part of market professionals about problems in the market and with certain securities. A series of internal communications between S&P analysts reflects a cynicism among them even as it shows their realization of what was happening. One S&P analyst wrote to a colleague that a deal being reviewed was "ridiculous" and that "we should not be rating it." The other analyst responded, "We rate every deal. It could be structured by cows and we would rate it" (Lucchetti 2008).[46]

The e-mails between credit analysts reflect the conflicts with "issuer pays" and the pressure the analysts were facing from underwriters. The SEC investigation uncovered the following e-mails from Moody's analysts—April 2006: "I am getting serious pushback from Goldman on a deal that they want to go to market with today" and August 2006: "They've become so beholden to their top issuers for revenue they have all developed a kind of Stockholm syndrome which they mistakenly tag as Customer Value creation."[47]

Other e-mails offered stark evidence of concern. An analytical manager wrote, "Rating agencies continue to create [an] even bigger monster—the CDO market. Let's hope we are all wealthy and retired by the time this house of cards falters." However, the e-mails also reflected the analysts' concerns

[45]"Anatomy of a Financial Collapse," p. 121.

[46]Also see SEC 2008.

[47]This and the following quotations are available at http://articles.businessinsider.com/2010-04-23/wall_street/30050293_1_housing-crisis-cdos-ratings-agencies#ixzz2ADxz3uXp.

about losing business. A commercial mortgage analyst sent the following e-mail about an upcoming meeting on the tensions rising among analysts about the quality of the ratings and the pressure to keep business coming in: "We are meeting with your group this week to discuss adjusting criteria for rating CDOs of real estate assets . . . because of the ongoing threat of losing deals." By 2008, Moody's had downgraded 73% of the mortgage-backed instruments it had rated as AAA to junk.

The end result was a series of rule changes by the SEC. Some of the changes related to the processes for rating financial instruments, adequacy of staff and resources for the rating processes, the lack of publication of rating standards, and the absence of justifications for so-called out-of-model adjustments. Under the Credit Rating Agency Reform Act of 2006 [15 U.S.C. § 78o-7(c)(2)], however, the SEC is prohibited from regulating the rating process. The Dodd–Frank Wall Street Reform and Consumer Protection Act [15 U.S.C. § 78o-7(p)(1)(A)] includes several sections that affect the credit rating system, including providing for the creation of an Office of Credit Ratings within the SEC and authority for the SEC to promulgate rules on the involvement of sales and marketing employees in the rating process. Dodd–Frank also prohibits compliance officers from participating in the rating processes or in the development of rating methodologies. In addition, Dodd–Frank requires the rating agencies to submit reports annually on how conflicts are handled, including the departure of employees to work at entities that are subject to rating by the agency. These annual reports require the agencies to submit information on whether they follow statutory and regulatory policy when conducting business; how they manage conflicts of interests; how they implement ethics policies, internal supervisory controls, and governance; and how complaints are handled (Ellis, Fairchild, and D'Souza 2012). Finally, Dodd–Frank requires the SEC to conduct a study of the conflicts that could result from the "issuer pays" model for compensating the rating services.

Ironically, the credit rating agencies were created to provide some type of third-party, objective evaluation of securities as "nonspeculative." The Banking Act of 1935 required banks to hold only investments that could be certified by rating agencies as nonspeculative (Partnoy 2001). In 1975, the third parties required for certification of nonspeculative securities were required to be a Nationally Recognized Statistical Ratings Organization, a designation the government gave to only four rating agencies prior to 2007. Although other rating agencies exist, the market is dominated by Moody's, S&P, and Fitch Ratings. The intent was to have a third-party imprimatur for the rating of securities as investment grade that was comparable to the approval conveyed by a public accounting firm's declaration that it has audited a company's financial statements.

The issuer-pays compensation system, however, created the same types of conflicts that were present when auditors furnished consulting services to their audit clients. To please those who pay, the bias is for the news always to be positive. The ability of the rating agencies to provide objective and meaningful ratings is only as strong as the ability of those in the rating agencies to overcome being beholden to those who pay—the underwriters who wish to issue investment-grade securities. Candor is the victim of such conflicts.

Positions against Investors. In addition to the structural and process problems that emerged from the analysis of the subprime mortgage and securitization markets, other investment banking practices eroded public trust. In a frank and stunning memo written to Goldman Sachs clients in January 2010 that followed the 2008 collapse of the financial markets and the congressional hearings on what the firm perceived its fiduciary duty to be, Goldman Sachs admitted that it often made recommendations to clients that it had already positioned itself to profit from. The memo read, in part, "We may trade, and have existing positions, based on trading ideas before we have discussed those ideas with you."[48] The disclosure that Goldman might hold positions against client interests had appeared in the fine print in Goldman's marketing materials, but the memo represented the first time that Goldman had discussed the policy openly with its clients.

Goldman faced and settled SEC civil charges related to its Abacus CDO deal because of allegations that it made recommendations to clients to purchase CDOs even as it was positioning itself short on the instruments. Because Goldman knew what types of mortgages were being used in the pools, Goldman positioned itself short on the securities it was selling to its clients. Once again, the true feelings of those involved were found in their internal e-mails. Employees referred to the firm's CDO securities as "junk," "s_____," or "crappy."[49] When Goldman executives were asked during congressional hearings held on the 2008 market collapse about their internal negative characterizations of securities that were being touted and sold to their clients, a Goldman executive, David Viniar, responded, "I think that's very unfortunate to have on email." When his response elicited laughter in the hearing room, Viniar changed his answer to, "It's very unfortunate to have said that in any form."[50]

The congressional hearings brought to mind the Brandeis observations of 1914 of investment banks playing both sides. Senator Claire McCaskill (D,

---

[48]Andrew Ross Sorkin, "At Goldman, E-Mail Message Lays Bare Conflicts in Trading," *New York Times* (13 January 2010):B1.

[49]Michael M. Phillips, "Senators Seek, Fail to Get an 'I'm Sorry'," *Wall Street Journal* (28 April 2010):A3, A5.

[50]Phillips, "Senators Seek, Fail to Get an 'I'm Sorry'," p. A5.

Missouri) confronted Goldman Chairman Lloyd Blankfein as he testified before Congress, "It feels like you guys are betting on the game you're playing," and the securities law expert, John Coffee, said, "I think we're seeing another one of those periodic eruptions, because we see this story of investment bankers who seem to be playing both sides against the middle, and the investor looks like a sucker."[51]

Goldman's activities in working against its products and investors have been described as "Heads Goldman wins, tails you lose."[52] William K. Black at the University of Missouri at Kansas City wrote, "Every game has a sucker, and in this case, the sucker was not so much AIG [American International Group insurance company] as it was the U.S. government and the taxpayer."[53] In November 2009, Blankfein defended his firm's conduct in an interview with the *London Times* by stating that he was just a banker "doing God's work."[54]

The question is whether God was aware of both the recommendations Goldman was making to customers and the nature of the mortgage pools at the time.

The Auction-Rate Markets. The auction-rate securities market, which hit its peak in 2008, involved issues similar to those present in the investment trusts of the 1920s. Auction-rate securities are long-term investments that have a short-term twist: The interest rates or dividends they pay are reset at frequent intervals through auctions, which typically occur every 7, 14, 28, or 35 days. Wall Street firms, including Goldman, were able to profit from their participation in these markets by touting the securities as money market funds but with a higher yield. The firms' clients would bid on securities being sold through a monthly auction that the investment firms were conducting. What their clients did not know is that their own investment advisers were bidding up the value of the instruments. The prices were reset weekly on the basis of demand, but the investment firms were creating that demand through their bids, bids that they never intended to execute because their clients would always bid more. The investment firms were setting a floor for the prices of the securities they were selling even as they were encouraging their clients to get in on what appeared to be a thriving market.

When Goldman, the fifth largest underwriter of the market, pulled out, the market for these securities collapsed. Clients were left holding $40 billion

[51]David Lynch, "Goldman Hearings Strike a Defiant Note," *USA Today* (28 April 2010):1B, 2B.

[52]Robert Farzad and Paula Dwyer, "Not Guilty, Not One Little Bit," *BusinessWeek* (12 April 2010):31.

[53]Farzad and Dwyer, "Not Guilty, Not One Little Bit":32.

[54]John Arlidge, "I'm Doing 'God's Work'. Meet Mr. Goldman Sachs," London Times Interview, *Sunday Times* (8 November 2009):1.

in securities they had been told were as good as cash. Arthur Levitt, former chairman of the SEC, commented, "Very few issues have shaken public confidence in the integrity of our markets as much as this."[55]

Through legal action brought by New York Attorney General Andrew Cuomo, Merrill Lynch, Citigroup, UBS, Goldman, and others agreed to buy back their clients' auction-rate securities. Goldman, however, agreed to buy back only the auction-rate securities of its smaller investors. Goldman left its larger investors holding the unsellable securities.[56]

After the Financial Crisis

The collapse of the mortgage market in 2008 was followed not only by reforms but also by settlements. Since then, the securities markets, securities firms, and investors have been rocked by pension crises, problems involving so-called expert networks, and renewed insider trading.

Regulatory Reforms: Dodd–Frank and Investor Protection Changes. The Dodd–Frank Wall Street Reform and Consumer Protection Act was passed in 2010 and created the Financial Stability Oversight Council (FSOC) to monitor the safety of the investments and soundness of financial institutions. The "safety and soundness" concepts remain as elusive, however, as they were in 1966 when the first federal legislation that invested bank regulators with the same authority was passed. In addition, how the FSOC fits into the regulatory structure, including bank examiners, is unclear. The extent of the FSOC's authority to shutter banks is also unclear.

Dodd–Frank addresses investor protections and imposes some changes in determining who qualifies as an accredited investor (one who has accumulated a certain level of assets or earnings). In their zeal to sell securities to retail investors, many brokers, during the market run-up, cobbled together the value of investors' homes, cars, and, as one scholar noted, "dogs," to have them meet the accrediting standard (Johnson 2012). Dodd–Frank prohibits counting an investor's home in reaching the qualifying asset level.

Investor protection was increased under Dodd–Frank in relation to the longstanding practice of using arbitration to handle investor disputes with financial services companies. The changes permit the SEC now to limit or prohibit mandatory arbitration requirements for investors. Whether through FINRA or any other SRO, the SEC now has the authority to prohibit or limit these arbitration requirements when it deems such to be in the "public interest or for the protection of investors."[57]

---

[55]Liz Rappaport, "Goldman Balks at Helping Rich Clients Recover from 'Auction Rate' Securities," *Wall Street Journal* (14 August 2008):C1.
[56]Rappaport, "Goldman Balks at Helping Rich Clients . . ., " p. C1.
[57]Dodd–Frank §928.

The Dodd–Frank provision that addresses the silent-for-too-long issue in the financial markets is the whistleblower bounty program. The bounty, ranging from 10% to 30% of the SEC's recovery (in cases in which the sanctions are more than $1 million), can be claimed by a whistleblower who voluntarily provides the SEC with original information that leads to a successful enforcement action. SOX offered protection against retaliation; Dodd–Frank offers that protection plus a bounty. The final version of the SEC rules for implementing the whistleblower bounty program offers greater rewards to whistleblowers who try first to report the information through the company's compliance program.[58] They are still given full credit for providing original information internally if, again, an enforcement action is successful. The bounty program does not require that whistleblowers report internally first, however, to qualify for a reward.

Settlements. The investor litigation that resulted from the collapse of the MBS market is extensive, and the SEC's proposed settlements have reflected judicial frustration with the industry and its regulators. For example, a Citigroup prospectus indicated that the mortgages in the pools all had to meet Citi's lending standards, which simply was not true. The SEC's proposed settlement with Citigroup for this misrepresentation of how it selected MBS was rejected by a federal judge. The $285 million settlement is on hold as the SEC and Citigroup appeal the lower court's rejection. The information about the Citi mortgage selection process came to light through several whistleblowers. Richard Bowen, a senior banker at Citi, told the bank's then-chairman, Robert Rubin, that 60% of the mortgages in the pool were defective. Bowen offered his warning in 2006, but despite repeated warnings over the years, no action was taken except to fire Bowen in 2009.[59] Under regulatory reforms, such whistleblowers enjoy extensive protection and incentives.

The settlements of private lawsuits against the investment banks are at amounts nearly double the SEC settlements. Citi has also agreed to settle for $590 million the private suits against it for allegedly deceiving investors by hiding the extent of its toxic subprime debt. Other banks are settling similar cases as follows: Wachovia, $627 million; Bank of America, $624 million; and AIG, $719 million.[60]

Pension Problems. The fallout from the 2008 market collapse continues as of this writing, four years later, as the recession makes its slow, punishing,

[58]Release No. 34-64545; File No. §7-33-10, RIN 3235-AK78, "Implementation of the Whistleblower Provisions of Section 21F of the Securities Exchange Act of 1934": http://www.sec.gov/rules/final/2011/34-64545.pdf.

[59]William D. Cohan, "Rethinking Rubin," *Newsweek* (20 September 2012):61.

[60]Suzanne Kapner, "Citi to Settle Suit for $590 Million," *Wall Street Journal* (30 August 2012):C1.

domino-like trek through the economy. Pension plans, public and private, have experienced revenue shortfalls and reductions in benefit payouts. Municipal bankruptcies have followed as pension portfolio values dropped to one-half of their 2007 peaks.[61] The evaluation of the risk in the pension portfolios was less than candid, with the result that cities overpromised on pension payouts based on analysis of portfolio values. In many cases, the valuations of those portfolios were given with an eye toward continuing valuation work. If the valuation of the portfolios came back with a positive tale to tell, no adjustments to pension benefits, city budgets, or tax rates were needed. If valuations reflected market risk and lower values, however, adjustments would have to be made, with the accompanying political pain that has become more obvious since 2008.

Expert Networks and Insider Trading. Despite the attention focused on the analyst profession in the postregulatory phase of the 2008 collapse, a swing to squeaky clean behavior has not occurred. Analysts have remained at the center of criminal prosecutions for insider trading, charges that have resulted from the creation of expert networks. Expert networks came to be widely used after Regulation FD, which put a damper on firms being able to obtain material nonpublic information. The networks are primary research firms that connect buy-side investors, consultants, and business decision makers with industry experts. Expert networks operate globally, and consultations between expert network clients and experts take many forms—from meetings to e-mails.

A review of the guilty pleas, trials, and convictions for insider trading of those in the same profession during 2012 indicates that little has changed. Only the methodology is slightly different. The expert networks and their interconnections with research firms and hedge funds, for a time, spawned a near-daily announcement of insider trading charges (Jennings 2010c). "They met at an analysts' conference" was ubiquitous in the news articles that covered nearly two years of insider trading arrests and resulting "perp walks" of hand-cuffed analysts, company executives, hedge fund owners, and members of expert networks.[62]

For example, federal criminal charges brought against analysts Don Chu and James Fleishman of Primary Global Research allege that their company received soft dollars in exchange for their ability to connect brokers' clients with outside experts.[63] And Primary Global Research was not an isolated

[61]Gunz and Jennings (2011); R. Eden Martin, "Unfunded Public Pensions: The Next Legal Quagmire," *Wall Street Journal* (19 August 2010):A17.

[62]James Bandler and Doris Burke, "Dangerous Liaisons at IBM," *Fortune* (26 July 2010):67, and Michael J. de la Merced and Zachary Kouwe, "Arrest of Hedge Fund Chief Unsettles the Industry," *New York Times* (19 October 2009):B1.

[63]Evelyn M. Rusli, "Amid Insider Trading Inquiries, Experts Get a Cold Shoulder," *New York Times* (28 December 2010):B4.

rogue company. The U.S. Attorney for the Southern District of New York has referred to insider trading using expert networks as "rampant."[64] But those within the profession continue to see this industry practice differently: "It's a legitimate business that walked a fine line."

What was being done in these cases was substantially different from the actions in the *Dirks* case of 1983. There is not much room for debate as to whether the crime of insider trading has been committed when analysts in research firms were contacting and compensating employees working within companies for material inside information about their companies. Using expert networks is different, at least theoretically, however, because the idea is to obtain general background information on industries and issues, not on specific company performance expectations.

When a company employee gives company information to an analyst who receives it and offers payment and then passes that information along to fund managers, the labels are, respectively, "tipper," "tippee 1," and "tippee 2." The addition of the label "research network" to the activity does not change that legal characterization. There is a difference between researching an industry and obtaining company-specific information on earnings and potential problems in, for example, drug research results from a pharmaceutical employee. The legal standard in such a situation is unequivocal. To show how far the tentacles reached to "experts" and then back to analysts and fund managers, the *Wall Street Journal* depicted the Galleon cases, to be discussed shortly, as a web.[65] All of the charges in the cases resulted in either guilty pleas or guilty verdicts.

In a throwback to the wiretaps that netted Boesky in the 1980s, wiretaps were again used to establish the crime and the intent of this new kind of insider trading. The indictments in the cases reveal phone conversations indicating that those involved were worried about their conduct. The indictment against analyst Don Chu (who entered a guilty plea to charges of insider trading) includes the following statement, obtained from a wiretap of his phone, of a call from him to fund manager Richard Lee (who has also entered a guilty plea to charges of insider trading): "Just talk . . . don't, don't put it down in writing. Dangerous . . . I'm nervous."[66]

---

[64]This and the following quotation are from Adam Shell, "Crackdown on Insider Trading Enters 'New Phase,'" *USA Today* (26 November 2010):1B.

[65]Susan Pulliam and Jenny Strasburg, "Consultant of 'Expert Network' Is Probed," *Wall Street Journal* (30 November 2010):C1—announcing the questioning of a consultant for the Gerson Lehrman Group.

[66]Peter Lattman and Azam Ahmed, "Executive Arrested in Trading Inquiry," *New York Times* (25 November 2010):B1.

The list of funds involved in investigations for the use of expert networks is long and distinguished.[67] "Everyone," across industries, was indeed providing or using expert networks. An examination of this round of insider trading, with analysts at the center, illustrates the role that ethics can play in reining in behavior. The founder of Galleon Group, Raj Rajaratnam, in an interview with federal officials who would make recommendations regarding the length of his sentence, offered the following:

> In my own mind, the line between permissible "detective work" and impermissible insider trading was not always clear, especially with regard to companies broadly covered by the news media as to which there was a wealth of publicly available information, including frequent leaks, rumors, and speculation about corporate transactions and other important developments.[68]

What had really happened in his mind is that he had crossed enough lines and conjured up sufficient rationalizations to find it difficult to distinguish between, on the one hand, legitimate research and, on the other hand, having a board member call you with advance notice of the company's earnings. He had slipped so far in his justifications that he was unable to see that paying company employees for inside information about upcoming financial quarterly reports was different from public information and leaks. Detective work does not include systematic payments to employees of companies for advance information. He had slipped, but he had failed to recognize the slippage as it carried him from research to felonies over a period of a decade. His presentencing report referred to him as "defiant," and he received the maximum sentence.

Common Threads of the Eras and the Ethical Way Forward

In 1996, an AIMR survey indicated that 86.6% of analysts believed that the senior managers of their firms seek high ethical standards for all employees (Veit and Murphy 1996). There was a disconnect, however, between that overall observation and what the analysts had actually been experiencing in

---

[67]Hedge funds that have been served with subpoenas in the insider trading investigations include Level Global Investors of New York; Diamondback Capital Management of Stamford, Connecticut; SAC Capital; and Loch Capital Management of Boston. Galleon Group, a hedge fund that is now defunct, was one of the initial targets in the insider trading investigation. See Peter Lattman and Azam Ahmed, "F.B.I. Raids Offices in Trading Inquiry," *New York Times* (23 November 2010):B, and Peter Lattman and Azam Ahmed, "SAC Capital and Two Mutual Funds Are Subpoenaed," *New York Times* (24 November 2010):B1. Mutual funds that have received subpoenas include Wellington Management Company and Janus Capital Group.

[68]David Glovin, "Galleon's Rajaratnam May Face Stiffer Jail Sentence after Questioning Law," *Bloomberg News* (12 September 2011): http://www.bloomberg.com/news/2011-09-12/galleon-s-rajaratnam-says-he-s-not-clear-on-insider-rules-u-s-says.html.

doing their jobs. For example, 24.1% reported that someone in their firm had acted unethically, but only 41.1% made a superior aware of the conduct. And 23% indicated that they had been asked in the past year by a member of senior management to do something illegal or unethical. Their attitudes about the profession also belied their relatively positive perspective on senior management. For example, 34.9% believed that ethical behavior had deteriorated in the past 10 years and only 24.3% believed it had improved.

The types of ethical issues that one-third of the respondents had observed periodically were (with only some seeing the behavior frequently and even fewer saying that they had never seen the issues)

- failing to use diligence and thoroughness in making reports (most common at 49%);
- writing reports that support predetermined conclusions;
- communicating inside information;
- trading on insider information;
- not dealing fairly with clients when taking investment actions;
- plagiarizing another's work;
- misrepresenting a firm's past or expected future performance;
- front running (making personal trades before client trades); and
- failing to disclose conflicts of interests.

The analysts who responded to the survey in 1996 listed no new categories of ethical issues—all of them were evident in the eras discussed previously. In fact, Leviticus, Rashi, and Hammurabi pretty much described it all with the apt description of placing stumbling blocks in front of the blind. Nor is there anything on the list that has not occurred again since 1996. Therein lies the rub: Why do the missteps recur? From tulips to railroads to reply stamps, the stories repeat.

One reason documented by this historical review is that we have not learned history's lessons. Another reason, evident in the examples in this historical review, is that the legalistic focus blinds professionals to higher ethical standards.

For example, at the Senate hearings on the 2008 market collapse, Senator Susan Collins of Maine posed a question to several Goldman executives,

> I understand that you do not have a legal fiduciary obligation. But did the firm expect you to act in the best interests of your clients as opposed to acting in the best interests of the firm? Could you give me a yes or no to

> whether or not you considered yourself to have a duty to act in the best interests of your clients?[69]

Fabrice Tourre, the young manager who was responsible for one of the collapsed Goldman mortgage funds, responded only with, "I believe we have a duty to serve our clients well."

When Lloyd Blankfein was confronted with the same question, he responded,

> While we strongly disagree with the SEC's complaint [a complaint the firm would later settle], I also recognize how such a complicated transaction may look to many people. To them, it is confirmation of how out of control they believe Wall Street has become, no matter how sophisticated the parties or what disclosures were made. We have to do a better job of striking the balance between what an informed client believes is important to his or her investing goals and what the public believes is overly complex and risky.

Other Goldman executives responded to Senator Collins with equally intriguing notions: "It's our responsibility . . . in helping them transact at levels that are fair market prices and help meet their needs" and "Conceptually, it seems like an interesting idea."

The legalistic approach cannot prevent the next clever trick that the financial markets develop to gain at the expense of customers. Each era brought regulation, which took hold only long enough for the next era to be ushered in with its new approaches and the same resulting harm to investors. Senator Phil Gramm once told Arthur Levitt, who was at the time SEC chairman, "Unless the waters are crimson with the blood of investors, I don't want you embarking on any regulatory flights of fancy" (Seligman 2003, p. 744). In other words, regulation is too little, too late. History shows that the cleanest period in the financial markets was when the profession was most active in the development of the profession. Following the post-1929 market collapse, the professionals in the investment markets stepped in voluntarily to make changes beyond the requirements of the new federal legislation. Stung by the public perception and the harm to their reputations, they organized, set professional standards, and through 1987, continued their steady growth and involvement. After 1987, there is a significant drop-off in discussion by the FAF, ICFA, AIMR, or CFA Institute in the literature. The leadership role of this group of professionals waned following the Boesky and Milken eras. Following consolidations of the groups and the creation of AIMR (later CFA Institute), however, the profession experienced a reinvigoration in terms of professional activity as well as in the literature. Professional practice and

[69]The material cited from this investigation is from "Wall Street and the Financial Crisis: The Role of Investment Banks," Hearings of the Permanent Subcommittee on Investigations (27 April 2010).

research activity increased. The CFA Institute *Standards of Practice Handbook* (2010) expanded in length, examples, and detail. The knowledge mission was evident in the quality of the *Financial Analysts Journal* as well as in the CFA Institute–sponsored seminars and education efforts through its Research Foundation.

The quasi-regulatory private bodies have remained in the background, however, except when an individual with blatant disregard of ethics appeared in a public report. Joel R. Blumenschein was banned by FINRA from running his firm for three months for his failure to supervise a broker who placed more than half of a customer's $80,000 retirement savings into penny stocks.[70] FINRA's complaint also accused Blumenschein of giving "evasive and contradictory" testimony to FINRA investigators.

Blumenschein accepted full responsibility for the broker's actions and the sanctions but continued to serve on FINRA's board. Other directors raised the question of whether Blumenschein could continue to serve, debated the issue, and then allowed him to remain on board. Their reasoning was that the discipline was not a license-stripping offense and only being stripped of one's license requires resignation from the board.

Such sophisticated rules interpretation, in lieu of a simple ethical standard, raises problems. The simple questions of, How will this look to the public? In the newspapers? How will the investor who lost money feel? were not asked. The conclusion that his offenses were "small potatoes reflected a lack of introspection as well as an ethical tin ear."[71] Continuing focus on the interpretation of rules cannot solve the types of ethical issues documented throughout the history of markets.

When the profession stepped into the regulatory frays following market collapses, the typical reaction was to resist. For example, in 1994, SEC Chairman Arthur Levitt proposed adding public representatives to the Financial Accounting Foundation because he believed the group was beholden to special interests. Levitt was trying to change the FASB rule on stock options, and FASB declined to do so. The Financial Accounting Foundation's control of FASB funding was the underlying concern. The political battles eclipsed discussion of the issues.

Indeed, the lapse in involvement of professional groups remains one of the unexplored causative factors in the market collapses across the eras. As for analysts, the groups had become no longer like the founders of the Financial Analysts Federation in Chicago, New York, Toronto, and so on, in the 1920s–1940s, whose discussions tended to introspection about the workings of markets, human nature, and ethics.

[70]Jean Eaglesham, "Finra Director Calls It Quits," *Wall Street Journal* (2 May 2012):C1.
[71]Eaglesham, "Finra Director Calls It Quits":C2.

Today, CFA Institute is taking the types of steps to restore trust in the profession that the founding members would recognize. The CFA Institute publication "50 Ways to Restore Trust in the Investment Industry" is an example of the concrete steps necessary to change behavior and prevent history's repetitious market cycles.[72]

This qualifies for 2.5 CE credits.

[72]http://www.cfainstitute.org/about/vision/serve/Pages/integrity_list.aspx?intCamp=hompage_banner_integrity_list.

Bibliography

Arbogast, Stephen V. 2009. "Commentary on Legal and Managerial 'Cultures' in Corporate Representation." *Houston Law Review*, vol. 46, no.1:33–59.

"This Commentary gets at some of the deeper roots that have prevented attorneys from properly advising their clients. The Commentary touches on specific attorney–client cases taken from both the Enron files and the Wall Street insider trading scandal of the late 1980s. These cases will illustrate both the influence of the structural-market issues and also certain successes experienced by attorneys who found means to overcome these forces. Ultimately, the goal is to make individual attorneys, law firms, and clients more aware that the corrupting influences on their relations are powerful, that they have deep roots, and that both additional safeguards and better personal formation are required if they are to be mitigated." (p. 33)

Bailey, Steve, and Steven Syre. 1996. "Taking Analysts' Tempting Forecasts with a Grain of Salt." *Boston Globe* (23 October):C1.

The article offers a note of caution about the use of analysts' reports because of the conflicts of interests and analysts' failures to issue sell recommendations when they were clearly warranted.

Barber, Brad, Reuven Lehavy, and Brett Trueman. 2007. "Comparing the Stock Recommendation Performance of Investment Banks and Independent Research Firms." *Journal of Financial Economics*, vol. 85, no. 2 (August):490–517.

"This study compares the profitability of security recommendations issued by investment banks and independent research firms. During the February 1996–June 2003 period, the average daily abnormal return to independent research firm buy recommendations exceeds that of the investment banks by 3.1 basis points, or almost 8 percentage points annualized. In contrast, investment bank hold and sell recommendations outperform those of independent research firms by 1.8 basis points daily, or 4.5 percentage points annualized. Investment bank buy recommendation underperformance is concentrated in the subperiod subsequent to the NASDAQ market peak (March 10, 2000), where it averages 6.9 basis points per day, or slightly more than 17 percent annualized. More strikingly, during this period those investment bank buy recommendations outstanding subsequent to equity offerings underperform those of independent research firms by 8.7 basis points (almost 22 percent annualized). Taken as a whole, these results suggest that at least part of the underperformance of investment bank buy recommendations is due to a reluctance to downgrade stocks whose prospects dimmed during the early 2000's bear market, as claimed in the SEC's *Global Research Analyst Settlement*. Additional analyses find that the underperformance of investment bank buy recommendations extends not only to the ten investment banks sanctioned in the research settlement but to the nonsanctioned investment banks as well." (p. 490)

Bauman, W. Scott. 1980. *Professional Standards in Investment Management*. Charlottesville, VA: Financial Analysts Research Foundation.

This work is one of the earliest studies on the commitment of financial analysts to professionalism in their practices and the maintenance of high standards of conduct in the public interest. The study reports the actual standards of conduct of 1,044 financial analysts as self-reported. Between 1980 and 1994, this study was the only one of four on ethical standards as practiced by analysts.

Bernstein, William J. 2006. "Corporate Finance and Original Sin." *Financial Analysts Journal*, vol. 62, no. 3 (May/June):20–23.

"The unique characteristics of the financial services industry present practitioners with challenging ethical demands. Of these, the potential for extraordinary monetary gain and the moral anesthesia resulting from the inward-looking nature of the profession conspire to hamstring effective regulation by industry insiders. Effective control of the industry must come from outside the industry. The choice is between regulation by a private entity and regulation by a governmental body." (p. 20)

Blume, Marshall E. 1993. "Soft Dollars and the Brokerage Industry." *Financial Analysts Journal*, vol. 49, no. 2 (March/April):36–44.

"Large investors frequently receive some type of research service in return for sending an equity trade to a specific brokerage firm. The commissions so directed are associated with the term 'soft dollars.' A survey of institutional managers and analysis of their trading records reveal something about the effects of soft dollars on the structure of the brokerage industry. The use of soft dollars has had significant effects on order flows to different types of brokers.

In particular, substantial percentages of the responding institutional managers indicated that soft dollars led them to use brokers they would not otherwise use. The evidence also indicates that the managers look to brokers providing soft-dollar research for execution of their easier trades, but continue to rely for their harder orders on traditional brokers willing to commit capital to facilitate trades. Respondents also indicated marked differences in their levels of satisfaction with trade execution according to the type of research purchased, with quality of execution for directed brokerage receiving the lowest marks." (p. 36)

Brandeis, Louis D. 1914. *Other People's Money and How the Bankers Use It*. New York: Frederick A. Stokes Company.

"After Wilson's election, Louis Brandeis (who was responsible for many of Wilson's ideas in the first place) wrote a series of articles for *Harper's Weekly* which outlined why the New Freedom was necessary and how best to implement it. In 1914, the articles were collected in book form and published under the title *Other People's Money and How the Bankers Use It*.

"Brandeis' central thesis was that the large banking houses were colluding with businessmen to create trusts in America's major industries. Brandeis felt that not only did trusts stifle competition, but also they became so large that they became unable to operate efficiently.

"Brandeis backed up his arguments with facts—copious facts gleaned from his battles against J.P. Morgan and Charles Mellen [sic] in the New Haven Railroad merger battle and from the Pujo Committee—a House committee report that investigated the abuses of the 'Money Trust.'

"Wilson was able to push through a number of laws regarding the regulation of business and trusts, but in many ways, due to mergers and stock manipulation, conditions in the business world today remain the same. Many of the details in *Other People's Money* may be dated, but its central ideas remain relevant—so much so that is still in print almost 90 years after it was first published." (This summary retrieved from Louis D. Brandeis School of Law, University of Louisville, webpage: http://www.law.louisville.edu/library/collections/brandeis/node/191.)

Bullock, Hugh. 1959. *The Story of Investment Companies*. New York: Columbia University Press.

This book is a popular history of U.S. investment companies (investment trusts). Bullock, an industry insider as head of Calvin Bullock, was an advocate for market growth as well as honesty and ability in market professionals. He was an advocate for such standards even before the 1929 crash and became more so after the crash. Bullock was described as a man whose word was his bond.

Burgunder, Lee B., and Karl O. Hartmann. 1986. "Soft Dollars and Section 28(e) of the Securities Exchange Act of 1934: A 1985 Perspective." *American Business Law Journal*, vol. 24, no. 2 (June):139–177.

This piece explores the enormous rise in securities trading volume during the 1981–1985 period and the resulting explosion in the amount of commission dollars available to investment managers for buying certain products and services from their brokers. Attracted by this rich source of capital, a variety of new firms entered the brokerage business to compete for these funds. In addition, the clients of the money managers became aware of the potential uses of the commission dollars generated by the investment of their assets and began to demand that services be purchased for their own accounts rather than for the use of money managers. Together, these competitive forces resulted in many questions about the extent of what products and services come within the statutory definition of research. Who must deliver these services to the money manager? Is a money manager protected if the manger's client tells the manager to direct the securities business to a particular broker? The piece answers these and other questions and is prescient in its analysis of the investment industry in the future.

Caccese, Michael S. 1997. "Ethics and the Financial Analyst." *Financial Analysts Journal*, vol. 53, no. 1 (January/February):9–14.

"Ethics is becoming an increasingly important aspect of our business and professional concerns. One reason is a growing emphasis on personal responsibility. Another is that ethical practices are good business." (p. 9)

CFA Institute. 2004. "CFA Institute Soft Dollar Standards." Charlottesville, VA: CFA Institute (http://www.cfapubs.org/doi/pdf/10.2469/ccb.v2004.n1.4005).

This book is a guide for ethical practice in relation to soft dollar charges and receipt of soft dollar benefits. The first standards were adopted in 1997, and the CFA Institute guidelines have evolved to include more details, including illustrations in this latest publication on the topic.

———. 2010. *Standards of Practice Handbook*. 10th ed. Charlottesville, VA: CFA Institute.

"The *Standards of Practice Handbook* (*Handbook*) provides guidance to the people who grapple with real ethical dilemmas in the investment profession on a daily basis; the *Handbook* addresses the professional intersection where theory meets practice and where the concept of ethical behavior crosses from the abstract to the concrete. The *Handbook* is intended for a diverse and global audience: CFA Institute members navigating ambiguous ethical situations; supervisors and direct/indirect reports determining the nature of their responsibilities to each other, to existing and potential clients, and to the broader financial markets; and candidates preparing for the Chartered Financial Analyst (CFA) examinations." (From "Preface," p. v)

Coffee, John C. 2002. "Understanding Enron: It's About the Gatekeepers, Stupid." *Business Lawyer*, vol. 57, no. 4 (August):1403–1420.

"Characteristically, the professional gatekeeper essentially assesses or vouches for the corporate client's own statements about itself or a specific transaction. This duplication is necessary because the market recognizes that the gatekeeper has a lesser incentive to lie than does its client and thus regards the gatekeeper's assurance or evaluation as more credible. To be sure, the gatekeeper as watchdog is typically paid by the party that it is to watch, but its relative credibility stems from the fact that it is in effect pledging a reputational capital that it has built up over many years of performing similar services for numerous clients. In theory, such reputational capital would not be sacrificed for a single client and a modest fee. Here, as elsewhere, however, logic and experience can conflict. Despite the clear logic of the gatekeeper rationale, experience in the 1990s suggests that professional gatekeepers do acquiesce in managerial fraud, even though the apparent reputational losses seem to dwarf the gains to be made from the individual client.

"Why has there been an apparent failure in the market for gatekeeping services? This brief comment offers some explanations, but also acknowledges that rival explanations lead to very different prescriptions. Thus, the starting point for responding to the Enron debacle begins with asking the right question. That question is not: Why did some managements engage in fraud? But it is rather: Why did the gatekeepers let them?" (pp. 5–6 of article)

Curry, Timothy, and Lynn Shibut. 2000. "The Cost of the Savings and Loan Crisis: Truth and Consequences." *FDIC Banking Review*, vol. 13, no. 2 (December):26–35.

This piece provides the backdrop for and cost of the savings and loan crisis of the 1990s. From the abstract: "The thrift cleanup was Congress's response to the greatest collapse of U.S. financial institutions since the 1930s. From 1986 to 1989, the Federal Savings and Loan Insurance Corporation (FSLIC), the insurer of the thrift industry, closed or otherwise resolved 296 institutions with total assets of $125 billion. An even more traumatic period followed, with the creation of the Resolution Trust Corporation (RTC) in 1989 and that agency's resolution by mid-1995 of an additional 747 thrifts with total assets of $394 billion. The combined closings by both agencies of 1,043 institutions holding $519 billion in assets contributed to a massive restructuring of the number of firms in the industry. From January 1, 1986, through year-end 1995, the number of federally insured thrift institutions in the United States declined from 3,234 to 1,645, or by approximately 50 percent."

Dash, Mike. 2000. *Tulipomania: The Story of the World's Most Coveted Flower & the Extraordinary Passions It Aroused.* New York: Crown Publishers.

"In the 1630s, visitors to the prosperous trading cities of the Netherlands couldn't help but notice that thousands of normally sober, hardworking Dutch citizens from every walk of life were caught up in an extraordinary frenzy of buying and selling. The object of this unprecedented speculation was the tulip, a delicate and exotic Eastern import that had bewitched horticulturists, noblemen, and tavern owners alike. For almost a year rare bulbs changed hands for incredible and ever-increasing sums, until single flowers were being sold for more than the cost of a house. Historians would come to call it tulipomania. It was the first futures market in history, and like so many of the ones that would follow, it crashed spectacularly, plunging speculators and investors into economic ruin and despair." From "Book Description" found on Amazon.com (http://www.amazon.com/Tulipomania-Coveted-Extraordinary-Passions-Aroused/dp/060980765X)

Day, Christian C. 2008. "Risky Business: Popular Images and Reality of Capital Markets Handling Risk: From the Tulip Craze to the Decade of Greed." *Pennsylvania State Law Review*, vol. 113, no. 2:461–526.

"Speculators are often portrayed in popular culture as predatory business people. Sometimes they are seen as fools. But, the portraits are often ill-informed. This article studies speculation found in Tulip Mania and the South Sea Bubble. The article then focuses on speculation in debt from the American Revolution. The Gilded Age and railroad building are surveyed. The article concludes with the Decade of Greed, the 1980s, as envisioned in film. While popular portraits are entertaining, the historic and economic reality is much different. Speculators play an important role providing capital and liquidity, risk taking, and rationing of resources critical for market economies." (p. 461)

Dennis, Kia. 2009. "The Ratings Game: Explaining Rating Agency Failures in the Build Up to the Financial Crisis." *University of Miami Law Review*, vol. 63, no. 4 (July):1111–1150.

This article posits that the rating agencies' underestimation of the risks of mortgage-backed securities was an economically rational response to legal, regulatory, and market incentives. In particular, revenues from rating MBS and other structured finance products grew exponentially between 2001 and 2006, so much so that by 2006, these ratings accounted for a significant part of rating agencies' total revenues. At the same time, however, the costs of inaccurate certification were declining as a result of judicial and regulatory actions favoring limited rating agency liability. As a consequence, the benefits of overrating MBS were greater than the costs of doing so. With this as a basis for understanding rating agency behavior in the months and years preceding the credit crisis, the article comments on the proposed regulatory overhaul and suggests that additional liability be imposed on rating agencies.

Dillon, Patrick, and Carl M. Cannon. 2010. *Circle of Greed: The Spectacular Rise and Fall of the Lawyer Who Brought Corporate America to Its Knees.* New York: Broadway Books.

Bill Lerach, who was the leading class-action securities lawyer in the United States, is now a convicted felon for paying off lead plaintiffs in the case. The stories in this book cover his class-action suits for shareholders of Enron, Disney, Apple, Time Warner, and others. He secured large recoveries for shareholders, but the book offers a portrayal of the risks in this form of recovery for shareholders.

Dirks v. SEC II. 1982. 681 F.2d 824.

This appellate decision resulted when analyst Raymond Dirks appealed the SEC sanctions against him for alleged insider trading in using information he obtained about fraud at Equity Funding in order to bring it to light even as he protected his clients by issuing a "sell" advisory.

Dirks v. SEC. 1983. 463 U.S. 646.

This U.S. Supreme Court decision reversed the sanctions imposed on analyst Raymond Dirks for using information he had obtained about Equity Funding to have his clients sell off their shares before the fraud became public.

Dooley, Michael P. 1980. "Enforcement of Insider Trading Restrictions." *Virginia Law Review*, vol. 66, no. 1 (February):1–83.

This pre-reform article argues for a less broad application of the insider trading standards and suggests that Congress actually intended Section 16 to be the section used to regulate insiders. The argument is that insider trading should be focused on and limited to fraud and manipulation and not be used for broader use of market information.

Dorfman, John R. 1997. "All-Star Analysts 1997 Survey: Sixteen All-Stars Excel for Fifth Time." *Wall Street Journal* (19 June):R1.

The *Wall Street Journal* annually reviews how analysts' recommendations compare with market performance. It looks at their techniques and accuracy. This article is one of the reviews.

Eichenwald, Kurt. 2005. *Serpent on the Rock.* Trade paperback ed. New York: Broadway Books.

This book provides a look at the Enron era market collapse and the issues that analysts and investors missed in the market run-up. From the preface: "As I covered the unfolding Enron and WorldCom scandals for the *New York Times* . . . I could not help but think that we as a nation we're reaping what we sowed. The outrage at Prudential had been just one in a long series of warnings about weaknesses in our financial system, signals that had all too long been ignored. I am something of a fatalist on this issue—as long as big money can be made from fraud, corporate scandals will always be with us. But even I would have thought that the embers from Prudential would have long been cooled before the next fire was lit. For all my pessimism, I was too optimistic.

"Why did we learn nothing? Why did corporate America continue down this self-destructive path?" (From "Preface" to 2005 trade paperback edition, p. xi. First edition published 1995.)

Ellis, Charles D. 2011. "The Winners' Game." *Financial Analysts Journal*, vol. 67, no. 4 (July/August):11–17.

"Practitioners of the investment management profession are underperforming for their clients and for their profession because of three errors: defining their mission as 'beating the market,' allowing the values of their profession to be eclipsed by the economics of the business, and not providing much-needed investment counseling. The solution is to incorporate investment counseling into the heart of their client–manager relationship." (p. 11)

Ellis, Nan, Lisa M. Fairchild, and Frank D'Souza. 2012. "Conflicts of Interest in the Credit Rating Industry after Dodd–Frank: Continued Business as Usual?" *Virginia Law & Business Review*, vol. 7, no.1 (Spring):1–46.

"Not surprisingly, investigations into the causes of the GFC [global financial crisis] have resulted in regulatory reform. These include reforms intended to address the conflicts of interest found within the CRA [Credit Reform Act] business model. In this Article, we evaluate these reforms. To accomplish this objective, in Part I, we provide an overview of CRAs including how conflicts of interest arise from their business practices; we also outline the role that CRAs played in the GFC and how conflicts of interest provided incentives encouraging inaccurate ratings. In Part II, we outline the lack of regulatory oversight prior to the Dodd–Frank Wall Street Reform and Consumer Protection Act ('Dodd–Frank'). We then, in Part III, analyze the adequacy of the provisions in Dodd–Frank intended to address conflicts of interest. We conclude that recent reforms are inadequate because they essentially allow for "business as usual" and allow CRAs to continue operating in a manner that facilitates conflicts of interest. Specifically, the reforms do nothing to address the issuer-pays business model which is ultimately the source of the multiple conflicts of interest. Until the issuer-pays model is eliminated, we believe CRAs will not provide accurate assessments of the creditworthiness of debt issuers in an impartial manner. As such, in Part IV, we outline additional reforms that are needed to eliminate these conflicts of interest. In particular, we advocate replacing the existing issuer-pays business model with a 'fee from proceeds' model that would eliminate the conflicts of interest within the CRAs and would lead to trustworthy credit ratings. Hence, we conclude by offering a detailed proposal to change the business model. We believe this model is essential to mitigate problems arising from conflicts of interest." (p. 1)

Evans, Cheryl. 2012. "What Makes You So Special? Ending the Credit Rating Agencies' Special Status and Access to Confidential Information." *Valparaiso University Law Review*, vol. 46, no. 4 (Summer):1091–1137.

"This Note argues that the big three credit rating agencies should be required to operate by the same rules as other financial market analysts and not receive selective access to confidential information. This special treatment has created a 'moral hazard' that endangers our entire financial system and must be eliminated.

"This Note begins in Part II by describing the structure of U.S. financial markets, the credit rating industry, the importance of ratings to the financial markets, problems associated with permitting the rating agencies to access confidential information, and the Dodd–Frank Act. Part III of this Note analyzes how the new Dodd–Frank Act addresses some of the problems that have plagued the credit rating industry and examines the unintended consequences and shortfalls of this legislation. Finally, Part IV of this Note advocates that the playing field should be leveled and the credit rating agencies should be required to operate like other investment analysts by ending their special status and access to confidential information. This change will eliminate the special distinctions accorded this cartel, help erase anticompetitive practices, lead to better credit ratings, and foster stronger financial markets." (From "Introduction," pp. 1094–1095)

Federal Reserve Data. 2004–2009. 1.54 Mortgage Debt Outstanding. Data from 2004 to December 2008 are in the Statistical Supplement to the Federal Reserve Bulletin (http://www.federalreserve.gov/pubs/supplement/default.htm). Data from January 2009 are published here: http://www.federalreserve.gov/econresdata/releases/mortoutstand/current.htm.

These data provide a year-by-year summary of mortgage debt and default rates.

Fels, Rendigs. 1949. "The Long-Wave Depression, 1873–97." *Review of Economics and Statistics*, vol. 31, no. 1 (February):69–73.

"Economic literature more often than not regards the period 1873–97 in America as a long-wave depression. Such an interpretation rests on two facts. First, the trend of wholesale prices was downward during the period, and reversed itself immediately afterward. Second, there was an unusually large number of depressed years compared to the periods before and after.

"There has consequently been a tendency to regard 1873–97 as comparable with the depressed years of the 1930s and to explain both periods on the same grounds. Such comparisons create misleading impressions. The purpose of this note is to correct such impressions and to introduce into the discussion some factors ordinarily given insufficient attention." (p. 69)

Francis, Jennifer, Qi Chen, Donna R. Philbrick, and Richard H. Willis. 2004. *Security Analyst Independence.* Charlottesville, VA: Research Foundation of CFA Institute.

"Many investors perceive, based primarily on anecdotal evidence, that analysts do not act independently. What the authors of this Research Foundation monograph provide is a scientific exploration of the evidence on the nature and causes of security analyst conflicts. They first investigate the conventional view that analysts are optimistic in their forecasts of earnings. They then explore the extent to which this optimism is associated with employer incentives, the influence of corporate managers, and the influence of fellow analysts. This comprehensive and insightful analysis should help investors evaluate the integrity of sell-side research and help regulators adopt wise policies."

Frantz, Douglas. 1987. *Levine & Co.: Wall Street's Insider Trading Scandal.* New York: Henry Holt.

Dennis Levine, a managing director of Drexel Burnham Lambert, was eventually sentenced to two years in federal prison for securities fraud, income tax evasion, and perjury. He flew to the Bahamas to pass along inside information to his co-conspirators in an insider trading ring that included Ivan Boesky. His sentence was less than his colleagues in fraud because he turned state's evidence and gave federal agents all they needed to know about those he called. This remarkable story describes how a young man was taken in by the draw of Wall Street power and rewards.

Freeman, Richard B. 2010. "Reforming the United States' Economic Model after the Failure of Unfettered Financial Capitalism." *Chicago-Kent Law Review*, vol. 85, no. 2:685–717.

"This Article is based on the 2009 Kenneth M. Piper Lecture at the Chicago-Kent College of Law. The 2008-2009 financial meltdown and ensuing economic developments have shown three things about modern capitalism: First, that unfettered financial markets remain the Achilles heel of capitalism with the capability of destroying economic stability and bringing misery to all. Second, that high-powered incentives paid to 'talent' in finance are a fundamental cause of the excessive risk-taking, chicanery, and financial fraud that contributes to instability. Without a new compensation system that rewards banking and finance for contributing to sustainable economic progress rather than for economic rent-seeking and a renewed regulatory system that punishes chicanery and financial crime and near-crime, there is unlikely to be any change in the behavior of the financial world. And finally, that in the wake of the implosion of laissez faire finance, labor and allied groups have to participate in rewriting the rules and regulations governing banking and finance so that finance serves the real economy rather than the reverse. Accordingly, if Wall Street insiders continue to make the key policy decisions alone, banking and finance will remain a loose cannon on the good ship Capitalism, sure to crash the ship yet again." (p. 685)

Galbraith, John Kenneth. 1954. *The Great Crash 1929.* New York: Houghton Mifflin Harcourt.

"Punctuated with wit and irony, Professor Galbraith's account of the stock market crash of 1929 is as fascinating as it is informative. Although written primarily for the layman, the book should be of considerable interest to economists. Galbraith denies that the crash was simply a belated and secondary result of depression forces already at work. Galbraith focuses on excessive speculation as the cause." [summary by Lorne D. Cook]

Gunz, Sally, and Marianne M. Jennings. 2011. "A Proactive Proposal for Self-Regulation of the Actuarial Profession." *American Business Law Journal*, vol. 48, no. 4 (December):641–711.

This article examines the way in which an actuary delivers services in the context of the pension funding crises that exist today, particularly in the United States, and also looks at the parallels between the functions, practices, and services of the actuary and those of the audit profession. Part I addresses the nature of the services provided by actuaries and their respective professional responsibilities. Part II details existing regulation, and Part III reviews the present pension crisis. Finally, Part IV offers proposals for self-regulatory mechanisms to address the practices within the profession that have been identified as factors that contributed to the present crisis in pension funding. Behavior by pension sponsors and their experts that has met minimum legal standards but resulted in funding shortfalls has created present and future funding crises for pensions and risk for beneficiaries. Without the profession imposing reforms that address the drivers of the behavior and the resulting funding gaps, the insolvency of pension funds will continue to be a risk and a reality.

Hill, Charles. 2002. Testimony Given at "The Watchdogs Didn't Bark: Enron and the Wall Street Analysts" Hearing before the U.S. Senate Committee on Governmental Affairs, 107th Congress (27 February):54–55 (http://www.gpo.gov/fdsys/pkg/CHRG-107shrg78622/pdf/CHRG-107shrg78622.pdf).

> This testimony of Charles L. Hill, director of research at Thomson Financial/First Call, documents the lack of resources and pressure felt by analysts as they grappled with the high volume of reviews for mortgage-backed securities.

Hong, Harrison, and Jeffrey D. Kubik. 2003. "Analyzing the Analysts: Career Concerns and Biased Earnings Forecasts." *Journal of Finance*, vol. 58, no. 1 (February):313–351.

> "We examine security analysts' career concerns by relating their earnings forecasts to job separations. Relatively accurate forecasters are more likely to experience favorable career outcomes like moving up to a high-status brokerage house. Controlling for accuracy, analysts who are optimistic relative to the consensus are more likely to experience favorable job separations. For analysts who cover stocks underwritten by their houses, job separations depend less on accuracy and more on optimism. Job separations were less sensitive to accuracy and more sensitive to optimism during the recent stock market mania. Brokerage houses apparently reward optimistic analysts who promote stocks." (p. 313)

Houck, Davis W. 2002. *FDR and Fear Itself: The First Inaugural Address.* College Station, TX: Texas A&M University Press.

> In Franklin Roosevelt's 1933 inaugural address, he called for substantial reforms of the stock market and indicted the ethics of those who were underwriting and selling securities.

Jarrell, Gregg A. 1984. "Change at the Exchange: The Causes and Effects of Deregulation." *Journal of Law & Economics*, vol. 27, no. 2 (October):273–312.

> "This paper presents some new evidence on the consequences of NYSE deregulation. The methodologies of finance are applied to time series of NYSE trading volume, returns to NYSE seats, returns to publicly traded NYSE brokerage firms, and quarterly income data on NYSE member firms. I find that NYSE volume after 1975 exceeds its predicted levels (based on a Box–Jenkins time-series model) but that NYSE seat values decline dramatically, even after accounting for the increased volume. The income data confirm the conclusion that deregulation in general reduced the profitability of the brokerage industry. But the publicly traded national brokerage firms benefited significantly, according to their stock returns. I also try to explain deregulation as a rational political response to an increasing elasticity

of demand of institutions for NYSE brokerage services. Using a political support theory adapted from those developed by Stigler and Peltzman, I show that the emergence of low-cost, off-board alternatives to block trading on the NYSE, and the acceptance by regional exchanges of large financial institutions as members, prove to be the forces responsible for deregulation." (p. 273)

———. 1989. "The Insider Trading Scandal: Understanding the Problem." In *Ethics and the Investment Industry*. Edited by Oliver F. Williams, Frank K. Reilly, and John W. Houck. Savage, MD: Rowman & Littlefield.

The author argues that each time regulators attempt to regulate market behavior, they actually "create large benefits for the very community of investment bankers and arbitrageurs from whose ranks the SEC has snared its impressive cast of convicted or accused criminals." (p. 85)

Jennings, Marianne M. 2003. "Restoring Ethical Gumption in the Corporation: A Federalist Paper on Corporate Governance—Restoration of Active Virtue in the Corporate Structure to Curb the 'Yeehaw Culture' in Organizations." *Wyoming Law Review*, vol. 3, no. 2:387–511.

"The Sarbanes–Oxley Act of 2002, variously known, as it swept through Congress, as the Public Company Accounting Reform and Investor Protection Act of 2002, Corporate and Auditing Accountability, Responsibility, and Transparency Act of 2002, Corporate Responsibility Act, the Corporate Fraud and Accountability Act, Justice for Victims of Corporate Fraud Act, the Corporate and Criminal Fraud Accountability Act, the Public Company Accountability Act, and just generally as 'What on earth were you people thinking when you decided to engage in this kind of financial reporting and analysis? Act.' Sarbanes–Oxley marks the third great regulatory reform for publicly held companies during the span of my 25-year career in the academy. First, there were the new laws and reforms on insider trading and junk bonds following the Ivan Boesky and Michael Milken debacles. Then there were the reforms that came about as a result of the collapse of savings and loans. 'Never again,' those responsible for these reforms and legislation muttered. With new requirements, new sanctions, new penalties, new public disgrace, no one would ever be so bold as to perpetrate schemes and artifices on the market ever again.

"Yet, here we are again. And we are tackling the same sort of task: How do we prevent corporations from trotting down these temporarily lucrative paths of fraud? What types of checks and balances could we create that would prevent such frauds, or, if fraud cannot always be prevented, human nature being what it is, what could we implement to insure that someone within the corporation raises the flag of fraud before the corporation hits Chapter 11? What type of governance creates the gumption needed in employees to step up and signal that there is fraud in the air and/or books? Indeed, why have we not been able to preserve in the corporate structure the fundamental ethical values of honesty and fair play? How was it possible to have corporations fully committed to values such as preservation of the environment, promotion of diversity, philanthropic contributions, and community service even as they were fully derelict in honoring Aristotelian values? A paraphrase of Dr. Stanley Milgram's work on delivering shocks as a group to individuals is in order, 'What is it about corporations that allows them to slip the restraints of human conscience?'

"Answering these questions requires an exploration of the debacles of this era. That exploration zeroes in on the vulnerable areas of the corporation and what factors contribute to employees', officers', directors', and auditors' disregard of virtue. Those areas of vulnerability are then addressed in a proposal for changing corporate governance so as to restore active virtue of ethical gumption in employees, officers, directors, and auditors, or that rare ability to speak up when debits become credits, losses become earnings, margins become inexplicable, bubbles become busts, and dreams turn to dust." (p. 387)

———. 2004. "A Contrarian's View: New Wine in Old Bottles, New Economy and Old Ethics—Can It Work?" In *Social, Ethical and Policy Implications of Information Technology*. Edited by Linda Brennan and Victoria Johnson. Hershey, PA: IGI Global.

This article takes a look at the similarities in ethical dilemmas across the eras of business and technological development. The conclusion of the piece is that ethical standards do not change; only the factual patterns differ. Principles that are simple and straightforward always apply to ethical dilemmas, but moral clarity is lost when new technology is used as a justification for departing from the basics of honesty, fairness, and forthrightness.

———. 2005. "Ethics and Investment Management: True Reform." *Financial Analysts Journal*, vol. 61, no. 3 (May/June):45–58.

"What happened to ethical behavior in the era of the dot-com, the bubble, Enron, and WorldCom? We were not involved in close ethical calls in these cases. The lapses were great, the conflicts many, and the cost, in terms of investor trust, nearly unspeakable. Each time scandals occur, market reforms result, but the pattern is that, despite their extensive nature, the reforms do not bring us an insurance policy against misconduct. True reform lies not in statutory or codified detail. Rather, true reform comes from a strong moral compass that is applied by leaders who demonstrate ethical courage. True reform requires a focus on doing more than the law requires and less than the law allows." (p. 45)

———. 2007. "Come See the Harder Side of Soft Dollars." *Corporate Finance Review*, vol. 11, no. 4:44–48.

"Money managers have fiduciary duties to their clients, the folks whose money they are managing. Fiduciary duty, translated loosely from legalese, means that the manager must act in the clients' best interests and not profit at the expense of the client. Fiduciary duty also means that the manager must make wise investment decisions for clients as well as arrange for others to carry out the transactions that are part of the investment strategy and decisions. However, around 1975, there was an uproarious scandal when clients discovered that their money managers were frequently paying commissions that were in excess of the lowest rate and, in many cases, the market rate. The free exchange of information has suffered, and market forces have been usurped, because of the presence of soft dollars and resulting cozy relationships between fund managers and broker/dealers. Investment managers can survive without the surreptitious relationships and perks of soft dollars. With disclosure, the markets will have the ability to evaluate the abilities of analysts, analysts who perform their work without the disclosed and undisclosed conflicts." (p. 44)

———. 2008. "How Did We End Up in This Spot?" *Corporate Finance Review*, vol. 13, no. 2:36–40.

"Ralph Cioffi and Matthew Tannin were bright and capable hedge fund managers at Bear Stearns. The fund was highly leveraged; the ration was about $20 borrowed for every $1 invested. The fund did very, very well through 2006, with a 40% return in one year. The fund was based on subprime mortgages, a market that was booming throughout 2006. If for no other reason, the fund managers owed it to their clients to be able to explain accurately the level of risk to which they were exposed. Tannin believed they should shut down the fund. His concerns should have been explored as a valid dissenting opinion. Even with those doubts expressed—low probability though they may have been—they continued to sell investors on the fund. Behaving as if the low probability did not exist resulted in higher risk. This is not about mismanagement of a hedge fund investment strategy. It is about premeditated lies to investors and lenders. As in all cases in which professionals are indicted, there are those signals along the way. They are not faint signals; there is a pattern here that should be applied as a template in all those decision-tree moments of customer products and investor relations." (p. 36)

———. 2009. "Paying Attention to Our Steps and Those Signs Again." *Corporate Finance Review*, vol. 13, no. 5:40–45.

"There is a process in ethical lapses that begins slowly, expands, increases in speed, and then consumes. The analysis of that initial step is the real ethical issue. Think of the possibilities for having earnings appear better, however marginally, than they really were. One-time events can be reclassified. The classification of capital vs. ordinary expenses provides ample room for the gray area and a justification for change: The timing of shipments; the decisions on write-downs; the amount in litigation reserves. When to take a charge for anticipated expenses, and how much to take. The entire accounting process when there is a merger or acquisition and the wiggle room you have. What debt is disclosed and where. Even the accounting differences for income tax, sales tax, and then for investors takes us down a path where we may not be sure of the ethical lines any longer." (p. 40)

———. 2010a. "The Goldman Standards and Shades of Gray." *Corporate Finance Review*, vol. 15, no. 1:35–41.

"The earlier stodgy negotiable instruments market proved insufficient for Goldman Sachs, as the firm drifted from its basic roots in tangible one-on-one business loans and transactions to the more exotic financial instruments. It was in the late 1920s that Goldman made this strategic shift, and since then Goldman has operated in that gray area, an area where no prosecutor can pull together enough evidence to show even a violation of the law, let alone criminal intent. However, there is a problem with the gray area: Goldman has pushed so far for so long that it may have reached a point of critical mass that impacts trust, and trust is necessary for capital markets to function; indeed, necessary for that initial step of investment in those markets. Goldman's gray-area strategy may be too clever by half. Those gray areas have opportunity because others, while they may see the gray, choose to stay well within the bright white of the rules. But living in the gray means that if anything goes wrong in that territory, attention shifts back to all of the conduct of the firm. This article provides the historical perspective, one that shows that Goldman finds the gray area and uses it without answering one of the basic questions in ethical analysis: Who could be affected by my actions? When your own clients could be harmed by your conduct, the time has perhaps arrived for a refusal to harm a client. Goldman is on track for double-digit billions in earnings for 2010, so the moral case may not be compelling. But these undisclosed interrelationships, while profitable, dissipate the trust that is necessary for both markets and investors." (p. 35)

———. 2010b. "Is Acquittal the New Ethical Standard?" *Corporate Finance Review*, vol. 14, no. 4:43–47.

> "The past few years have handed us some landmark cases in finance and trading in which the acquittals seemed to defy facts. As with all the acquittal cases, there is indeed a fine line. That fine line is one drawn between gathering information (information obtained through the sweat of the brow) and obtaining and using inside information. When we are gauging behavior by the strict legal standards, we do come close to the edge of illegality. Rather than waiting for the knock, perhaps some introspection is in order. That's where ethics come in. Only worrying about *mens rea* and *actus reus* and proudly proceeding with 'prove it' often do win the day in court. And in the process we chip away at the transparency and forthrightness efficient markets require for long-term progress. But yes, you could do that. And yes, everyone does do that and it is standard industry practice. But should it be? This is the question that requires an answer if we would like to avoid having fraud become a routine market correction." (p. 43)

———. 2010c. "The Lessons from Galleon Hedge Fund and the Insider Trading Ring." *Corporate Finance Review*, vol. 14, no. 5:43–45.

> "Raj Rajaratnam, the former head of Galleon Group, now stands at the center of one of the SEC's largest insider trading rings since Ivan Boesky roamed Wall Street. In a classic tipper/tippee insider trading case, the SEC and the Justice Department have charged the principals of the Galleon Group with receiving information from insiders that they then used to position themselves profitably in the markets. There is a final ethical lesson for companies involved in trading information. The young trader at Galleon who was terminated for refusing to bend the ethics bar is perhaps the person who emerges from the Galleon web with the best credentials and the critical lessons. He knew that something was not quite right in that he was not making trades and money from superior skill, foresight, and industry. The companies with moles needed to step up, as Intel did in 2002 with Ms. Khan, and explore, investigate, and enforce. When analysts' predictions are eerily close, the time has come for an internal look at what employees are doing. Insider trading requires someone who wants the information and someone on the inside willing to sell. Prosecutors handle the discipline for those seeking the information. However, they require companies' assistance in rooting out those within who are disseminating the information. Companies have the tools and access to do so without a warrant and may represent a key prevention point in the web-like growth of deceit of companies such as Galleon." (p. 43)

———. 2011a. "Does Dodd–Frank Countermand Sarbanes–Oxley? On Whistle-Blowers and Internal Controls." *Corporate Finance Review*, vol. 16, no. 1:41–44.

> "What happens when Dodd–Frank meets Sarbanes–Oxley? Time will provide complete answers, but there is on the surface of the two bulky statutes a conflict. That conflict may interfere with a corporation's ability to have employees use internal reporting mechanisms. Under Dodd–Frank, those who report to the Securities Exchange Commission (SEC) a company's violation of federal securities law are entitled to collect not less than 10% and up to 30% of all monetary recovery (including damages, fines, and any other monetary sanctions) in the event the SEC is able to successfully litigate or settle charges brought against the whistleblower employee's company that are based on the information provided by the whistleblower. To prevent Dodd–Frank rewards from trumping 404 self-discovery, CFOs must now assume a new role of trusted confidant. If employees trust those in charge and feel their concern, and concern does breed loyalty, even the 30% statutory reward will not countermand the hard work of 404 self-repair unless employees' issues fall on deaf ears and result in inaction." (p. 41)

———. 2011b. "The Irony of Complicity: Lehman Brothers, Ernst & Young, and Repo 105." *Corporate Finance Review*, vol. 15, no. 6:36–41.

> "The former executives of Lehman Brothers will likely not face criminal or civil charges with regard to their remarkable accounting. While one member of Congress has said that Lehman's accounting was about as close to fraud as you can get, the SEC officials have let it be known that they are doubtful that the executives broke any federal laws. No Wells notices have been issued to any of the former Lehman executives or to Ernst & Young, the defunct firm's auditor at the time of the controversial use of Repo 105. However, Ernst & Young faces the state attorney general of New York who concludes that Repo 105 was a house-of-cards business model, designed to hide billions in liabilities in the years before Lehman collapsed. The Repo 105 maneuver allowed Lehman to sell off its instruments for cash; cash that was then used to pay down Lehman's debts. Spinning things off the books begins with small steps of technical compliance with accounting and financial reporting standards, but detracts from the business operations and then deteriorates into a dependence on the accounting sleights-of-hand, a nonsustainable business model. Auditors need to look beyond technical compliance to the firm's true financial performance and its future vulnerability once the dependence on financial techniques begins." (p. 36)

Johnsen, D. Bruce. 1994. "Property Rights to Investment Research: The Agency Costs of Soft Dollar Brokerage." *Yale Journal on Regulation*, vol. 11, no. 1:75–113.

The author provides a full history of NYSE trading, including a look at the drivers for eliminating fixed commissions as well as the growth of mutual funds and the need for fund managers' access to research.

Johnson, Jennifer J. 2012. "Fleecing Grandma: A Regulatory Ponzi Scheme." *Lewis & Clark Law Review*, vol. 16, no. 3:993–1013.

"This Article examines the regulatory failure that allowed Medical Capital to engage in a Ponzi scheme to market over $2 billion in promissory notes as private placements. Utilizing a vast stockbroker network, Medical Capital sold the notes to more than 20,000 retail investors including vulnerable senior citizens. The Article explains how in spite of many warning signs, none of the potential gatekeepers, including the SEC, FINRA, the stockbrokers, the banks, the attorneys, or the independent due diligence analyst interceded to protect the investors.

"Under current SEC rules, issuers can sell any dollar amount of private placement securities to an unlimited number of defined accredited investors with virtually no governmental oversight. The Article recommends that in line with its authority under the Dodd–Frank Act, the Commission tighten the standards for accredited investor status. The Article further argues that, coupled with untethered stockbroker activity, the current regulatory structure unduly favors small business at the expense of retail investors. This problem will be exacerbated by the 2012 JOBS Act, which mandates looser advertising rules for Rule 506 private placements. The Medical Capital fraud suggests that Congress and the SEC are misguided in their heavy reliance upon stockbrokers as effective intermediaries. The Article concludes with a modest proposal to rein in the activities of the brokers." (p. 993)

Katz, Jonathan. 2010. "Reviewing the SEC, Reinvigorating the SEC." *University of Pittsburgh Law Review*, vol. 71, no. 3:489–516.

"The Securities and Exchange Commission (SEC) celebrated its 75th anniversary in 2009. Ordinarily this would be a basis for celebrating the triumphs of the agency. However, the financial crisis of 2008 and the celebrated frauds and failures of the immediate past have provoked a wealth of criticism of the SEC and calls for fundamental change in the operations of the Commission. An objective review of the history of the SEC demonstrates that the recent failures are not unique. In fact, for each of these notable scandals and failures there is an important historical parallel in the history of the SEC. While one might conclude from this recurring pattern of frauds and failures that no set of reforms will ever eliminate periodic financial disasters and frauds, this paper takes a different perspective. The recurring pattern may be evidence that there are fundamental characteristics of how the SEC functions that contribute to its historic tendency to wait for events to happen before acting. This paper identifies and discusses these elements of the Commission's 'DNA' and offers recommendations for change." (p. 489)

Langevoort, Donald C. 1990. "Investment Analysts and the Law of Insider Trading." *Virginia Law Review*, vol. 76, no. 5 (August):1023–1054.

"The thesis of this Essay is that the argument for special treatment of analysts under the insider trading rules, while not implausible, is substantially overstated. As articulated to date, the pro-analyst argument invokes an image of the process of investment analysis and its role in market efficiency viewed through rose-colored glasses, as if routine analyst activity has come to represent such exemplary behavior in an efficiency-driven model of the capital marketplace that idealization has foreclosed criticism. In fact, there is reason to doubt the strength of the efficiency claim, and cause for concern that, absent some form of restriction, conflicts of interest in the issuer–analyst relationship may lead to a troublesome bias in the way information will be allocated among analysts. We are left, then, with a considerable degree of ambiguity in policy formulation, weakening the claim for preferential treatment.

"Part I of the Essay provides a context for understanding the problem and states the argument for the analyst in greater detail. Part II considers the influence that the pro-analyst argument has had in producing a remarkable doctrinal change. Part III then reconsiders the argument, introducing a broader range of potential explanations for issuer–analyst behavior and exploring their consequences in light of insider trading theory. Finally, Part IV suggests some directions the law could take after a refined understanding of the problem." (p. 1023)

Leiser, Burton M. 1989. "Ethics and Equity in the Securities Markets." In *Ethics and the Investment Industry*. Edited by Oliver F. Williams, Frank K. Reilly, and John W. Houck. Savage, MD: Rowman & Littlefield.

Stock brokers and investment advisers are no more rapacious than their brothers and sisters in other lines of work, but the industry in which they work may provide unique opportunities for enormous profits for those who are sufficiently inventive and willing to take the necessary risks. Because creativity and risk taking are prominent characteristics of those who succeed as investment bankers, managers, and advisers, no one should be surprised to learn that those who are most successful in illegitimate activities have often been eminently successful and have made an important mark in their legitimate role as well.

Levitt, Arthur. 1999. "Best Execution: Promise of Integrity, Guardian of Competition." Presented to the Securities Industry Association, Boca Raton, FL (4 November): http://www.sec.gov/news/speech/speecharchive/1999/spch315.htm.

> "As markets around the world continually evolve, the commitment to integrity, and the innovation spurred by competition among market centers, will be our twofold competitive edge. The stakes have never been greater for America's markets. We simply cannot afford to let our competitive edge be dulled.
>
> "In today's dynamic environment, the duty of best execution presents brokers with new and difficult challenges. I recognize that many of you in this room have risen to meet these challenges, that you strive daily to ensure that your customers receive the execution they deserve. I commend you for your individual and collective efforts.
>
> "I worry, however, that the duty of best execution is being neglected by those who fail to review carefully their order routing arrangements. I worry that best execution may be compromised by payment for order flow, internalization, and certain other practices that can present conflicts between the interests of brokers and their customers.
>
> "Are conflicts in the order routing and execution process diluting the natural forces of competition in our markets—reducing price competition and isolating pools of liquidity? The investor interest, the integrity of our markets, and the future of our global preeminence demand that we face these questions, and that we resist any erosion in the duty of best execution.
>
> "This is a critical time to ask: What does the fundamental obligation of best execution mean in today's markets and in the markets of tomorrow—regardless of what form they take?"

Lin, Hsiou-wei, and Maureen F. McNichols. 1998. "Underwriting Relationships, Analysts' Earnings Forecasts, and Investment Recommendations." *Journal of Accounting and Economics*, vol. 25, no. 1 (February):101–127.

> "We examine the effect of underwriting relationships on analysts' earnings forecasts and recommendations. Lead and co-underwriter analysts' growth forecasts and recommendations are significantly more favorable than those made by unaffiliated analysts, although their earnings forecasts are not generally greater. Investors respond similarly to lead underwriter and unaffiliated 'Strong buy' and 'Buy' recommendations, but three-day returns to lead underwriter 'Hold' recommendations are significantly more negative than those to unaffiliated 'Hold' recommendations. The findings suggest investors expect lead analysts are more likely to recommend 'Hold' when 'Sell' is warranted. The post-announcement returns following affiliated and

unaffiliated analysts' recommendations are not significantly different." (p. 101)

Lucchetti, Aaron. 2008. "S&P Email: 'We Should Not Be Rating It.'" *Wall Street Journal* (2 August).

This article provides a summary of the incriminating and embarrassing e-mails written by credit rating agency analysts about their lack of information and time for evaluating instruments such as CDOs.

Macey, Jonathan R. 2004. "Efficient Capital Markets, Corporate Disclosure, and Enron." *Cornell Law Review*, vol. 89, no. 2:394–422.

"The collapse of Enron dealt a stunning blow, not only to people's wallets and a once-formidable U.S. corporation, but also to a number of conventional theories and core beliefs within the legal academy. The theories and beliefs challenged by the Enron debacle include the following: (1) the U.S. corporate governance system is the best in the world; (2) the U.S. system of corporate disclosure is the best in the world; and (3) the U.S. capital markets, particularly the markets for large corporations such as those listed on the prestigious New York Stock Exchange (NYSE), are highly efficient.

"Following a brief corporate history of Enron, Parts I, II, III, and IV of this Article discuss, in turn, what remains of each of these conventional academic theories in the wake of Enron's collapse. My principal conclusions are as follows: Initially, with respect to U.S. corporate governance, the collapse of Enron reveals the fundamental tradeoff between objective and proximate monitoring by corporate directors, auditors, rating agencies, analysts, and others. Second, the collapse of Enron demonstrates that disaster ensues when supposedly neutral and objective corporate monitors are "captured" by the firms they are supposed to monitor. Third, the U.S. system of corporate governance relies on these objective monitors more than other corporate governance systems, and is therefore more vulnerable when such monitors fail, as was the case with Enron. The downfall of Enron also illustrates both the importance of corporate governance to corporate performance, and the inherent susceptibility to corruption present in any system of corporate governance." (pp. 394–395)

Melville, Lewis. 1921. *The South Sea Bubble.* London: Daniel O'Connor.

This book tells the story of one of the market's earliest bubbles, which reflects uncanny similarities to the bubbles of the 20th and 21st centuries.

Michaely, Roni, and Kent L. Womack. 1999. "Conflict of Interest and the Credibility of Underwriter Analyst Recommendations." *Review of Financial Studies*, vol. 12, no. 4 (July):653–686.

"Brokerage analysts frequently comment on and sometimes recommend companies that their firms have recently taken public. We show that stocks that underwriter analysts recommend perform more poorly than 'buy' recommendations by unaffiliated brokers prior to, at the time of, and subsequent to the recommendation date. We conclude that the recommendations by underwriter analysts show significant evidence of bias. We show also that the market does not recognize the full extent of this bias. The results suggest a potential conflict of interest inherent in the different functions that investment bankers perform." (p. 653)

Mizruchi, Mark S., and Daniel Hirschman. 2010. "The Modern Corporation as Social Construction." *Seattle University Law Review*, vol. 33, no. 4:1065–1107.

"We argue that in the post–World War II period, a leading segment of the American corporate elite adopted a moderate, pragmatic approach that included an accommodation to government intervention in the economy and an acceptance of the rights of organized labor. We argue that the managerial autonomy spawned by the separation of ownership and control provided the conditions within which American corporate executives could engage in these policies. This system, however, began to break down in the 1970s, and a major acquisition wave in the 1980s brought stockholders back to prominence. Faced with pressures not seen since the early 1900s, corporate managers became increasingly shortsighted, and the corporate elite became increasingly fragmented. The result has been a business community unable to organize to address the problems of the 21st century in a way that its predecessors did in earlier decades. We conclude by discussing the implications of this argument for the thesis of *The Modern Corporation*." (p. 1067)

Morley, Alfred C. 1989. "Nurturing Professional Standards in the Industry." In *Ethics and the Investment Industry*. Edited by Oliver F. Williams, Frank K. Reilly, and John W. Houck. Savage, MD: Rowman & Littlefield.

The author provides a history of the beginning of professional groups and standards for participants in the investment markets. In particular, he documents the history of the CFA examination, including the ethical standards demanded.

Moses, Barbara. 2004. "They Were Shocked, Shocked: The 'Discovery' of Analyst Conflicts on Wall Street." *Brooklyn Law Review*, vol. 70 (Fall):89–115.

"This article accepts, in large part, the premises underlying much of the current criticism of sell-side analysts and their conduct during the 1990s: that the analysts were, in fact, operating within a system that subjected them to pervasive pressure to recommend stocks based on the needs of the investment banking divisions of the brokerage firms that employed them instead of the best interests of retail investors. Consequently, many analysts (though by no means all) issued overly-optimistic research reports pushing stocks that they privately doubted or even derided. Nonetheless, the flurry of editorializing, rulemaking, enforcement activity, and civil litigation that began in 2001 and went into high gear in 2002—all in response to what by then was called the analyst conflict 'scandal'—reminds this cynical observer a bit of the classic scene in Casablanca where Captain Renault, standing in front of the roulette wheels he has played for years, solemnly announces: 'I'm shocked, shocked to find that gambling is going on in here.'

"No securities regulator should have been shocked to discover that sell-side equity analysts were joined at the hip to their investment banking colleagues and that the objectivity of their research suffered as a result. To the contrary: Throughout the last decade, the pressures placed on analysts to favor the interests of investment bankers over the interests of investors were discussed frankly in the nation's financial press. Moreover, the fact that these pressures compromised the objectivity of the research product was well understood by sophisticated market participants. Indeed, in the late 1990s—well before Eliot Spitzer made headlines with his investigation of Merrill Lynch—at least two separate academic studies found that the recommendations issued by analysts working for firms with investment banking ties to the companies they covered were more positive, but less accurate, than the recommendations issued by their noncompromised colleagues.

"The empirical evidence also shows that the recommendations published by underwriter-affiliated analysts had less of an impact on market prices than recommendations authored by more independent analysts, meaning that the market discounted research likely to be biased. This in turn suggests that such research had less to do with the Internet bubble—and that the discovery of the bias had less to do with the bubble's collapse—than the current crop of class action plaintiffs and their lawyers would like to believe." (p. 89)

Murdock, Charles W. 2011. "The Dodd–Frank Wall Street Reform and Consumer Protection Act: What Caused the Financial Crisis and Will Dodd–Frank Succeed in Preventing Future Crises?" *Southern Methodist University Law Review*, vol. 64:1243–1325.

"The effectiveness of Dodd–Frank's response to the investment banks is somewhat mixed. The Act provides a modest risk retention requirement of 5% so that securitizers will have some 'skin in the game.' With respect to curbing excessive management risk taking, the Act relies upon disclosure and independent boards, neither of which has been highly effective in the past. The provisions dealing with inadequate capitalization and proprietary trading require extensive rule-making before their impact can be known. With respect to 'too big to fail,' Dodd–Frank does not deal adequately with the 'too big' aspect, but it does set up a mechanism to deal with failing institutions.

"Part VI deals with the credit rating agencies and how they lost their souls by valuing market share and growth over critical analysis. The impact of Dodd–Frank upon credit agencies should be very positive. It makes substantial structural and transparency changes and also clarifies that the credit rating agencies can be held accountable through private litigation, thereby undercutting the claim of such agencies that their ratings are protected by the First Amendment.

"Part VII examines the role of derivatives, both in creating the crises and prolonging it. It discusses the Goldman Sachs settlement when Goldman sponsored a synthetic CDO [collateralized debt obligation] without disclosing that the mortgages underlying the credit default swaps had in part been chosen by an investor who wanted to bet against the mortgages. The Article also asserts that credit default swaps should be prohibited because of the moral hazard and information asymmetry when a creditor, which has a due diligence obligation, buys protection from a third party. Moreover, the existence of naked default swaps magnified the impact of the subprime mortgage defaults.

"The Conclusion asserts that the Dodd–Frank Act should prevent a financial crisis in the future that mirrors the past crisis because it should markedly change lending practices. It should also put a stop to the shameful role of the credit rating agencies that went from serving as trusted analysts to wholesaling AAA ratings. The impact on the big banks, however, remains to be seen. With respect to 'too big to fail,' the Dodd–Frank Act fails to address adequately the 'too big' issue, namely, the ever increasing aggregation of financial power in large financial institutions. It does create, however, a sound mechanism to deal with systemically large institutions that may fail in the future. In addition, it does not adequately deal with the underlying issue that drives any financial crisis, management incentives that lead to excessive risk taking, nor does it reverse the increased concentration in the financial services industry." (p. 1243)

Oberlechner, Thomas. 2007. *The Psychology of Ethics in the Finance and Investment Industry*. Charlottesville, VA: Research Foundation of CFA Institute.

"Thomas Oberlechner applies concepts and findings from the field of psychology to develop a variety of methods for understanding, and teaching about, ethics in financial markets. To see why using psychology to understand financial ethics is almost imperative, let us momentarily force an ethical decision into the economist's standard model of a utility-maximizing individual.

"To decide whether to commit an ethics violation, such an individual has to estimate the expected utility of the financial gain from the unethical behavior. But that estimate is just a start. He or she also has to estimate the cost, which includes (1) the expected disutility of being caught, where the likelihood of being caught is also a factor, and (2) the disutility of having a guilty conscience. These last components are obviously psychological, and Professor Oberlechner's deep knowledge of the body of research in psychology—which is unfamiliar to most readers with only a finance education—makes his discussion of the connection between psychology and financial market ethics lively and informative." (From "Foreword" by Laurence B. Siegel, p. viii)

Padilla, Alexandre. 2008. "How Do We Think about Insider Trading? An Economist's Perspective on the Insider Trading Debate and Its Impact." *Journal of Law, Economics & Policy*, vol. 4, no. 2:239–262.

"This essay assesses what impact, following Henry Manne's publication of *Insider Trading and the Stock Market,* the insider trading debate had on how we think about insider trading. Using economic analytical tools, Manne's analysis shed new light on insider trading and gave a new breath to the insider trading debate. Manne's work opened venues to new analyses on insider trading from lawyers, economists, and financiers. This paper attempts to see if Manne's work has contributed to the change in lawyers' views toward insider trading but also the views by policymakers, lawmakers, and the general public." (p. 239)

Park, James J. 2012. "Rules, Principles, and the Competition to Enforce the Securities Law." *California Law Review*, vol. 100, no. 1:115–180.

"Rule-enforcement and principle-enforcement differ in terms of cost and controversy of enforcement. First, rule-enforcement is generally less costly than principle-enforcement. Rules have clearly defined meanings and are meant to be easily applied to specific situations. Principles, on the other hand, are vaguely defined and require substantial investment in investigation and litigation to enforce. Second, rule-enforcement is less controversial than principle-enforcement. Rule-enforcement tends to target technical violations of a regulatory scheme and is less likely to result in moral condemnation and significant sanctions for the violator. In contrast, principle-enforcement involves application of broadly worded provisions with disputed meanings to firmly sanction conduct that violates public values.

"Enforcers differ in their ability to take on the cost and controversy of principle-enforcement as well as the values that influence their enforcement of principles. Industry enforcers such as self-regulatory organizations (SROs) are more likely to focus on rule-enforcement and interpret principles narrowly in light of industry values, which value predictability and reliance on industry standards. A regulatory enforcer, such as the SEC, can find it difficult to aggressively enforce principles because its enforcement must be consistent with broader regulatory policy that reflects the work of an objective, expert regulator. Public-values enforcers, such as federal prosecutors and state attorneys general, are most likely to enforce principles aggressively in light of public values, but may be more likely to be influenced by politics than the SEC. Entrepreneurial enforcers, such as class action attorneys, have financial incentive to invest significantly in principle-enforcement, but also have incentives to bring questionable cases for profit. . . .

"This Article assesses this choice in the context of three enforcement models—consolidated, supervisory, and decentralized. Each model reflects different degrees of centralization and different tolerances for pluralism. The consolidated model, which would reduce the number of enforcers, has the advantage of reducing conflict among enforcers, but also eliminates enforcers who can act more aggressively in expressing public values than an expert enforcer. The supervisory model seeks to retain the advantages of having multiple enforcers while controlling them through supervision, but it is unclear that supervision would add much to what the courts already do in screening meritless cases. The decentralized model has the advantage of relying on a wide array of enforcers with different approaches and strengths but can cause conflict and is costly.

"This Article argues that the case for multiple enforcers is best made by emphasizing the comparative advantages of those enforcers, rather than focusing on whether an optimal amount of enforcement has been produced. Industry and regulatory enforcers are best at rule-enforcement, while public-values and entrepreneurial enforcers are best at principle-enforcement. Even if one enforcer could perform both enforcement roles, it might be more efficient for that enforcer to focus on what it does best. The SEC's expertise commits it to playing a particular role in the enforcement scheme that prevents it from effectively playing all roles. Reforms may be desirable in better defining the focus of different enforcers in order to reduce conflict between enforcers. Organizing securities enforcers in two tiers, one group focusing on rule-enforcement, the other group focusing on principle-enforcement, might be a way of managing the conflict that can result from multiple enforcers." (From "Introduction," pp. 119–120)

Partnoy, Frank. 1999. "The Siskel and Ebert of Financial Markets: Two Thumbs Down for the Credit Rating Agencies." *Washington University Law Quarterly*, vol. 77, no. 3:619–712.

"In this article, I argue that the paradox of rating agencies is best explained by the practice of linking substantive securities regulation to private credit ratings. I argue that, from the mid-1970s until today, the Securities and Exchange Commission (SEC) and other regulatory bodies, by promulgating rules that depend substantively on credit ratings, have given the handful of approved credit rating agencies . . . a substantial degree of market power. . . . Such regulatory licenses have benefitted rating agencies to varying degrees since the 1930s.

"I argue that the recent increase in the scope of these regulatory licenses not only has caused substantial deadweight loss due to the agencies' ensuing oligopoly, but also has encouraged the rating agencies to shift from the business of providing valuable credit information to the far more lucrative business of selling regulatory licenses. The new regulatory scheme has had dramatic effect, not only causing a decline in the informational value of credit ratings, but also creating incentives for the agencies to provide inaccurate ratings and for market participants to pay for regulatory entitlements stemming from the agencies' ratings, instead of paying for the informational content of the ratings. The result is a bewildering array of dysfunctional financial behavior as well as substantial financial market distortion and inefficiency. One prominent market participant aptly labeled these phenomena a 'chronic sickness' in the financial markets.

"The solution I offer for this problem is simple, perhaps bitter, medicine. The SEC and other regulatory agencies should remove each of these regulatory licenses by excising the portions of their rules that depend substantively on credit ratings. . . .

"In place of ratings-dependent regulation, I recommend a replacement: simply substitute credit spreads, the market risk measure of bonds, for credit ratings. Credit spreads are more accurate than credit ratings, and by definition credit spreads reflect the market price of credit, which should reflect at minimum the information contained in credit ratings." (From "Introduction," pp. 623–624)

———. 2001. "The Paradox of Credit Ratings." University of San Diego School of Law, Law and Economics Research Paper No. 20: http://papers.ssrn.com/sol3/papers.cfm?abstract_id=285162.

This paper concludes that credit ratings have scant informational value because the changes lag behind the market by months. Some institutions, however, cannot purchase certain securities without the ratings, no matter how invalid they are—hence, the paradox.

Pearce, Russell G., Steven H. Resnicoff, Mark A. Sargent, and W. Bradley Wendel. 2006. "Symposium Panel One: Does Corporate Decision Making Allow Room for Religious Values?" *Fordham Journal of Corporate & Financial Law*, vol. 11, no. 3:547–571.

The authors discuss Leon Festinger's theory of cognitive dissonance. They recount Festinger's theory: "Basically, he argues that if you are forced to do something that you feel is morally repugnant, you build up emotional dissonance; you become emotionally distressed. It is difficult to deal with doing something you think is wrong. Consequently, you try to find a way to escape, a way to avoid the unsavory conduct. But if as a practical matter you are unable to change your conduct, then you seek refuge from your cognitive dissonance by changing your opinions. What once seemed immoral now seems quite acceptable, perhaps even laudatory. Your views change because you have to cope with this emotional stress" (p. 559). This psychological phenomenon can cause professionals to engage in behavior that they believe to be ethically wrong and perhaps self-destructive.

Peck, Sarah. 2011. *Investment Ethics*. New York: John Wiley & Sons.

"*Investment Ethics* is an applied and uniquely focused textbook that provides readers with tools, examples, and exercises they need to understand ethical concepts and consequences in the practice of investments. The book . . . [is] a general introduction to ethics and ethical challenges facing investment professionals. [It] complements and reinforces concepts in Investment and Security Analysis by integrating ethical issues into the rigorous and applied analysis of subjects such as reporting risk–return measures of performance, trading practices, information and security prices, analysts' earnings forecasts, and fundamental security analysis.,

"The need for ethical education is as long standing as the history of scandals that plague the financial industry. Understanding the cause and effect of economic crises and scandals from an ethical perspective ensures the long run health of our financial markets. Sarah W. Peck's *Investment Ethics* is an applied and uniquely focused textbook that provides students with the tools, examples, and exercises they need to understand ethical concepts and consequences in the practice of finance; especially regarding investments. This text serves not only as a key tool in the classroom, but also a longstanding guide for examining the ethical practices of companies and organizations." (From "Overview" at http://www.wiley.com/WileyCDA/WileyTitle/productCd-EHEP001759.html)

Perino, Michael. 2010. *The Hellhound of Wall Street.* New York: Penguin Press.

"In *The Hellhound of Wall Street,* Michael Perino recounts in riveting detail the 1933 hearings that put Wall Street on trial for the Great Crash. Never before in American history had so many financial titans been called to account before the public, and they had come within a few weeks of emerging unscathed. . . . Pecora became an unlikely hero to a beleaguered nation. . . .

"By creating the sensational headlines needed to galvanize public opinion for reform, the Pecora hearings spurred Congress to take unprecedented steps to rein in the freewheeling banking industry and led directly to the New Deal's landmark economic reforms."

Pratt, Sereno S. 1905. "Our Financial Oligarchy: " In *The World's Work*, vol. 10. Edited by Walter Hines Page and Arthur Wilson Page. New York: Doubleday, Page & Company:6704–6714.

This chapter provides a look at early Wall Street and discusses issues of control of markets through a lack of transparency about market processes, conflicts, and positions.

Prince, J. Dyneley. 1904. "Review of *The Code of Hammurabi.*" *American Journal of Theology*, vol. 8, no. 3:601–609.

This review of the content of Hammurabi's code relates its application to our work today.

Regan, Nancy. 1987. *The Institute of Chartered Financial Analysts: A Twenty-Five Year History.* Charlottesville, VA: The Institute of Chartered Financial Analysts.

This book provides a sense of the history of the founding of the ICFA and the development of the CFA exam as well as standards for the profession and the expansion of educational and research opportunities. The book reflects the extent of the volunteer effort that went into the founding and refining of the CFA Program and the Research Foundation.

Rhodes, James Ford. 1906. *History of the United States from the Compromise of 1850 to the McKinley-Bryan Campaign of 1896*, vol. 7. London: Macmillan.

This general history contains perspectives on the development of the modern corporation and financial markets. It includes discussions of presidential views on markets and market regulation.

Ribstein, Larry E. 2006. "Imagining Wall Street." *Virginia Law & Business Review*, vol. 1, no. 2 (Fall):165–200.

"Oliver Stone's 1987 film *Wall Street* offers a particularly good lens through which to view Hollywood's treatment of business. The film's powerful images and characters, combined with the timing of its production and release, illustrate the potential political consequences of cinema in general, and movies dealing with business in particular. A documentary included on the DVD presents significant insight into the filmmakers' views. What emerges is a picture of a cultural phenomenon that was both perversely misguided about the business it portrayed and exerted a powerful influence on that business.

"*Wall Street* was the third film Oliver Stone directed, having previously won four Academy Awards (including Best Director and Best Picture) for his first film, *Platoon*. Although *Wall Street* was not nearly as successful as *Platoon*, selling only about a third as many tickets, its main character, Gordon Gekko, played by Michael Douglas in an Academy Award winning performance, became an icon of capitalism. The film has played a large role in the legal academic literature—Gordon Gekko has been mentioned in almost 60 articles in Westlaw's Journals and Law Reviews database. This is not surprising, since its literate and nuanced script penetrates deeper into the firm than any other major film." (p. 166)

Rosenberg, Irene Merker, and Yale L. Rosenberg. 1998. "Lone Star Liberal Musing on 'Eye for Eye' and the Death Penalty." *Utah Law Review*:505–539.

This historical look at the development of law and ethics includes reviews of religious and code effects on conduct and punishment.

Rozeff, M.S., and M.A. Zaman. 1988. "Market Efficiency and Insider Trading: New Evidence." *Journal of Business*, vol. 61, no. 1 (January):25–44.

"That corporate insiders earn profits from stock trading does not surprise most financial economists, but that outsiders can earn abnormal returns by using publicly available insider trading data constitutes a serious exception to stock market efficiency. We show that this anomaly continues to exist despite the publication of studies attesting to its existence. We suggest that the anomalous profits to outsiders are a manifestation of the size and earnings/price ratio effects. Controlling for these factors reduces outsider profits by half; the additional assumption of a 2% transactions cost makes outsider profits zero or negative. Insider profits from trading in shares of their companies are also greatly reduced. Insider profits after an assumed 2% transactions cost are a moderate 3% per annum for annual holding periods." (p. 25)

SEC v. Capital Gains Research Bureau, Inc., 375 U.S. 180 (1963). Citing Hanbury, *Modern Equity*, 8th ed. (1962):643. *See* Letter of Lord Hardwicke to Lord Kames, dated June 30, 1759, printed in Parkes, *History of the Court of Chancery*, (1828):508, quoted in Snell, *Principles of Equity*, 25th ed. (1960).

This U.S. Supreme Court case deals with the conduct of an analyst who was advising his clients to take one position in equity stock even as he took the opposite position in order to benefit from their naive reliance on him because of his lack of disclosure.

SEC. 2008. "Summary Report of Issues Identified in the Commission Staff's Examinations of Select Credit Rating Agencies." Washington, DC: U.S. Securities and Exchange Commission (July).

The report provides the SEC summary of the e-mails and other documents that indicate the understaffing, lack of resources, and skepticism of credit analysts as they attempted to cope with the deluge of offerings they were expected to rate without sufficient time and information. The summary of reforms is also included.

Seligman, Joel. 2003. *The Transformation of Wall Street*. 3rd ed. New York: Aspen Publishers.

In the third edition of this book, Seligman again draws on extensive personal interviews to provide a comprehensive examination of the origins, accomplishments, successes, and failings of the SEC from its creation in 1934 to the enactment of the Sarbanes–Oxley Act in 2002.

Sender, H. 1986. "What the Scandals Wrought." *Institutional Investor*, vol. 20 (October):243–245.

The article examines the damage from the junk bond era and the impact on investor behavior and trust.

Seyhun, H.N. 1986. "Insider's Profits, Costs of Trading, and Market Efficiency." *Journal of Financial Economics*, vol. 16, no. 2 (June):189–212.

"This study investigates the anomalous findings of the previous insider trading studies that any investor can earn abnormal profits by reading the *Official Summary*. Availability of abnormal profits to insiders, availability of abnormal profits to outsiders who imitate insiders, determinants of insiders' predictive ability, and effect of insider trading on costs of trading for other investors are examined by using approximately 60,000 insider sale and purchase transactions from 1975 to 1981. Implications for market efficiency and evaluation of abnormal profits to active trading strategies are discussed." (p. 189)

Siconolfi, Michael. 1992. "Under Pressure: At Morgan Stanley, Analysts Were Urged to Soften Harsh Views." *Wall Street Journal* (14 July):A1.

This article documents the interference from the IPO side of the investment house in the analyst side of the house so as to influence behavior, and it discusses the resulting pressure on analysts to amend their reports.

Simons, Michael A. 2002. "Vicarious Snitching: Crime, Cooperation, and 'Good Corporate Citizenship.'" *St. John's Law Review*, vol. 76, no. 4:979–1017.

> "Snitching—or, more euphemistically, 'cooperation'—has a long history in our criminal justice system. Judicial leniency for cooperators traces its roots back hundreds of years to the common law practice of approvement, and American prosecutors have been striking deals with cooperators since at least the 19th century. Over the past 15 years, however, federal criminal prosecutions have undergone what can fairly be characterized as a cooperation revolution. Ever since the advent of the Federal Sentencing Guidelines in 1987, defendants have increasingly seen cooperation as their best chance to avoid a stiff prison sentence, and prosecutors have increasingly relied on cooperators to make cases. . . .
>
> "This Article will examine corporate cooperation and the difficulties it can create for corporate decision-makers. Part I describes the principles of vicarious guilt that give prosecutors the power to demand corporate cooperation. Part II examines how prosecutors exercise their discretion in deciding whether to charge corporations with crimes. In Part III, the Article examines the cooperators. Just as a corporation's guilt is only vicarious, so too its cooperation can be only vicarious. In the end, it is not the corporation that cooperates, but its officers and directors—the men and women who make decisions for the corporation. For these vicarious snitches, the process can be a minefield, filled with conflicting loyalties and inevitable self-interest." (From "Introduction," pp. 979–982)

Stewart, James B. 1991. *Den of Thieves*. New York: Simon & Schuster.

> "*Den of Thieves* tells, in masterfully reported detail, the full story of the insider-trading scandal that nearly destroyed Wall Street, the men who pulled it off, and the chase that finally brought them to justice. Pulitzer Prize winner James B. Stewart shows for the first time how four of the biggest names on Wall Street—Michael Milken, Ivan Boesky, Martin Siegel, and Dennis Levine—created the greatest insider-trading ring in financial history and almost walked away with billions, until a team of downtrodden detectives triumphed over some of America's most expensive lawyers to bring this powerful quartet to justice.
>
> "Based on secret grand jury transcripts, interviews, and actual trading records, and containing explosive new revelations about Michael Milken and Ivan Boesky written especially for this paperback edition, *Den of Thieves* weaves all the facts into an unforgettable narrative—a portrait of human nature, big business, and crime of unparalleled

proportions." (Book Description found on Amazon.com at http://www.amazon.com/dp/067179227X)

Stoll, Hans R. 1979. *Regulation of Securities Markets: An Examination of the Effects of Increased Competition*. New York: New York University Press.

This book provides one of the first looks at the post-1975 markets, with the change in commission rates and the impact on competition when brokerage houses could charge higher commission rates. Stoll has remained a steady presence in the literature in terms of following market structural and regulatory changes and the resulting impact on competition.

Tarbell, Ida M. 1904. *The History of the Standard Oil Company*. New York: Macmillan.

A historian looks at the founding and growth of the Standard Oil Company.

Tett, Gillian. 2009. "Insight: A Matter of Retribution." *Financial Times* (3 September): http://www.ft.com/cms/s/0/f197ed60-98a5-11de-aa1b-00144feabdc0.html#axzz2UDrQJwSH.

This article provides a summary of the criminal and civil penalties that have been imposed as a result of the financial crises of the last 50 years.

Veit, Theodore E., and Michael R. Murphy. 1996. "Ethics Violations: A Survey of Investment Analysts." *Journal of Business Ethics*, vol. 15, no. 12 (December):1287–1297.

"The authors analyze the responses to a mail survey of securities analysts who were asked about their ethical behavior and the ethical behavior of people with whom they work. The findings show the types of ethical violations that occur and the frequency with which they occur. The findings also show how respondents deal with observed violations of ethical behavior. All responses are analyzed to determine if differences exist between the responses of analysts having different characteristics (gender, age, years of employment, and education), and differences in employment circumstances (firm size, firm type, buy side/sell side, U.S./Canada)." (p. 1287)

Walter, Ingo. 1991. *The Secret Money Market*. New York: HarperCollins.

The author takes a dark look at the markets, including insider trading, and discusses the power of market participants to influence market movements.

Williams, Oliver F., Frank K. Reilly, and John W. Houck, eds. 1989. *Ethics and the Investment Industry*. Savage, MD: Rowman & Littlefield.

This book is a report of the 1987 "Ethics and the Investment Industry" symposium at the Center for Ethics and Religious Values at the University of Notre Dame. Thoughtful scholars and practitioners offer their insights on financial markets, including essays on insider trading, takeovers, futures markets, nurturing professionalism in the industry, the ethics of equity, ethical perspectives of investment bankers, and religious hope in the investment industry. This book is a compelling set of essays that was prescient in its predictions of ethical issues that would arise as markets grew.

Zetlin, Minda. 1990. "Is Wall Street Really So Bad?" *Management Review*, vol. 79, no. 7 (July):1–33.

"In a period of less than 5 years, 2 Wall Street giants—Drexel Burnham Lambert and E.F. Hutton—lost their authority following a fraud conviction. Some observers feel that there are other companies on Wall Street that are rife with insider trading, fraud, and general moral bankruptcy. According to F.M. Scherer, a Swarthmore professor who has studied mergers, acquisitions, and selloffs at more than 4,000 companies, many acquired businesses are stripped of departments critical to a company's long-term growth in favor of a bigger, more immediate profit. If acquisitions were bad for a company, it seems logical that managers would eschew them. Unfortunately, some executives, seeing opportunity to make a large sum of money through an acquisition are not only [not] trying to prevent them but are actively taking part in their construction." (p. 1)

Made in the USA
Monee, IL
04 November 2026

67382316R00056